# Vedic Astrology and the Vedas

*An Intermediate Guide on Hindu Astrology & the Ancient Teachings of the Vedas. Decoding the Collection of Sacred Religious Texts of Wisdom, Tradition & Astronomy*

Manjula Tara

# Table of Contents

**Introduction** .................................................................. i

**Chapter 1: A Glimpse at Astrology Around the World** ............ 1
    **Reviewing Astrology** ................................................. 2
    **Eastern Astrology** ..................................................... 3
    **Western Astrology** ................................................... 4
    **Hindu Astrology** ....................................................... 5

**Chapter 2: An Introduction to the Vedas** ............................ 7
    **Revisiting the Vedas** .................................................. 7
    **The Rig-Veda** ............................................................ 10
    **The Sama Veda** ........................................................ 11
    **The Yajur Veda** ......................................................... 11
    **The Atharva Veda** .................................................... 11
    **Sruti vs. Smriti** ......................................................... 12
    **The Teachings of the Vedas** ...................................... 13

**Chapter 3: Vedic Teachings in the Modern World** ................ 17

**Chapter 4: The Vedas and Vedic Astrology** .......................... 27

**Chapter 5: Historical Figures in Vedic Astrology** ................... 33
    **Parasara Muni** .......................................................... 34
    **Vyasa** ........................................................................ 35
    **Lagadha** ................................................................... 36
    **Yavanesvara** ............................................................. 37
    **Brahmagupta** ........................................................... 38

| | |
|---|---:|
| Aryabhata | 39 |
| **Chapter 6: Creating Your Vedic Astrology Chart** | **41** |
| Creating Your Chart by Hand | 42 |
| The Houses | 45 |
| Reading the Signs in the Planets | 47 |
| Reading the Yogas | 48 |
| **Chapter 7: Using Your Vedic Astrology Chart** | **49** |
| Life Prediction | 50 |
| Marriage | 51 |
| To Understand Karma | 52 |
| To Understand Health | 53 |
| To Understand Finances | 54 |
| To Understand Family Life | 55 |
| To Understand General Skills | 56 |
| **Chapter 8: Reading Your Chart in the Sky** | **59** |
| Revisiting the Nakshatras | 60 |
|    Ashwini | 61 |
|    Bharani | 63 |
|    Krittika | 65 |
|    Rohini | 66 |
|    Mrigashira | 68 |
|    Ardra | 69 |
|    Punarvasu | 71 |
|    Pushya | 72 |
|    Ashlesha | 73 |
|    Magha | 75 |
|    Purva Phalguni | 76 |
|    Uttara Phalguni | 78 |
|    Hasta | 79 |

| | |
|---|---:|
| Chitra | 80 |
| Swati | 82 |
| Vishakha | 83 |
| Anuradha | 84 |
| Jyeshtha | 85 |
| Mula | 86 |
| Purva Ashadha | 88 |
| Uttara Ashadha | 89 |
| Shravana | 90 |
| Danishtha | 91 |
| Shatabhisha | 93 |
| Purva Bhadrapada | 94 |
| Uttara Bhadrapada | 95 |
| Revati | 97 |
| **Introducing the Yogas** | **98** |
| A Note on the Kendras | 99 |
| **Important Yogas** | **100** |
| Gaja Kesari-Yoga | 100 |
| Kedar Yoga | 101 |
| Kahal Yoga | 101 |
| Kamal Yoga | 102 |
| Musala Yoga | 102 |
| Neechabhanga Raja Yoga | 102 |
| **Auspicious Yogas** | **103** |
| Ruchaka Yoga | 103 |
| Bhadra Yoga | 104 |
| Hansa Yoga | 104 |
| Malavya Yoga | 104 |
| Sasa Yoga | 105 |
| **Inauspicious Yogas** | **105** |
| Kemdrum Yoga | 105 |
| Daridra Yoga | 106 |
| Grahan Yoga | 106 |
| Shakat Yoga | 106 |
| Chandal Yoga | 107 |

|  |  |
|---|---|
| Kuja Yoga | 107 |

## Yogas of the Sun
|  |  |
|---|---|
| Veshi Yoga | 107 |
| Vaasi Yoga | 108 |
| Ubhayachari Yoga | 108 |

## Yogas of the Moon — 108
|  |  |
|---|---|
| Sunafa Yoga | 109 |
| Anafa Yoga | 109 |
| Durudhara Yoga | 109 |
| Kema Druma Yoga | 110 |

## Planets in Constellations
|  |  |
|---|---|
| Sun | 110 |
| Moon | 116 |
| Mercury | 122 |
| Venus | 128 |
| Mars | 134 |
| Jupiter | 139 |
| Saturn | 144 |
| Rahu | 150 |
| Ketu | 155 |

# Chapter 9: Finding Your Partner With Vedic Astrology — 161

**Guna Milan** — 162

**Mangal Dosha** — 165

**Navamsa Chart Compatibility** — 168

# Conclusion — 171

# Introduction

People have always looked to the skies for history. People have always looked up to the heavens for answers to the mysteries of life. From being able to know what will happen, or understanding how to navigate through difficult situations, it is difficult for us to figure out what we are doing. It can be hard for us to know what will happen when we do not have any vision of the future. By looking to the skies, we start to see what may happen around us. This is because everything in the universe is connected. Our lives, the skies, the planets, and stars... It is all interrelated and all tangles together. When we do this, we can start predicting the future. We can see karmic ties and influences as the fruits of our karma eventually come to life.

History has taught people time and again to look up at the heavens. The heavens allow for karma to be read. They allow people to see what it is that they need to do. This art can be learned more and more. You can learn it by making sure that you know how to read the stars. You can start to see what the universe has in store for you. You can learn about your potential marriage matches. You can see how successful you may be so you can guide your own choices.

If you are interested in being able to learn about the world around you and if you are interested in being the person that you want to be, then you are in the right spot. Learning to acknowledge how everything ties together and connects is simpler than you probably thought. Being able to see how you can read the world around you will help you immensely. Knowing what you are doing and how to do it is the perfect way that you can start looking at the skies as well.

If you are brand new to Vedic Astrology, you may want to slow down and start off with a beginner's book. This is designed to be an intermediate guide, and while we will have brief recaps over certain concepts, for the most part, this book assumes that you have some basic understanding of core concepts. You will need that understanding if you want to be able to navigate, and if you can do that, you will have the understanding that you need.

As you read through this book, you will gain a menagerie of good information that will help you. We will begin by taking a look at astrology around the world. Eastern, Western, and Hindu astrology all vary in their own ways. Being able to see these differences will help you figure out what you are doing. We will be addressing the Vedas and looking at how important they are in understanding Vedic astrology, as well as focus on what they teach. Recognizing the influences of the Vedas will help you to get that solid foundation that will help you to see Vedic astrology through a clearer lens that will help you to better see the messages in the skies.

Now, in the previous book, we took the time to go over the understanding of a basic birth chart. Here, we will be going over-interpreting them a bit more thoroughly. We will go over how you can start calculating out your own. We will discuss how you can use that astrology chart yourself so you can use it to its fullest extent. The more that you do this, the more you will be able to tap into the karma that the world has set out for you.

We will also take a look at how you can read the sky. By looking at the various combinations of stars, constellations, and Planets in the skies, you will start seeing what the universe has in store for you. We will look at the various ways that you can expect the universe to influence you. We will start by looking at the lunar mansions in their four positions. We will also go over the most important yogas to understand as well. Some are important, and others are unlucky. Others still are related to the Sun and moon. These yogas are important to see as well, as when they form in your chart, they are incredibly powerful.

So, are you ready to begin seeing the truth? Are you ready to start taking a look at what the universe has in store for you?

# Chapter 1: A Glimpse at Astrology Around the World

Now, we have discussed a lot about Vedic astrology in the previous book. It is a form of astrology that is influenced highly by the Vedas. This particular form of astrology varies greatly from Western astrology, another point that we have discussed heavily in the previous book. However, if you wish to read your birth chart, it is probably a good idea to start by breaking down the differences between the various astrology that exist. Now, remember, though this book is focusing on Vedic astrology, it is not intended to create issues for those who follow Western astrology. Just because you are reading about or following the practices of Vedic astrology doesn't mean that you cannot also look at the other forms. In fact, you are strongly encouraged to explore other forms of astrology to figure out which ones are right for you at any point in time. The more that you can do this, the better you will do. The more that you learn about the skies, the more clearly you will be able to read the movements of the Planets and what they mean. This means that some of the best things that you can do to help yourself to understand Vedic astrology will be to learn as much as you can about other forms as well. You may find that you get very good insight through doing so, and that will help you immensely.

They are separate, but they are not contradictory. They have their own spins and nuances that will allow you to figure out what it is that will work best for you. Many times, people choose just one form of astrology that they choose to focus on, and it is quite likely that you will do so as well at some point. Whether you are still relatively new to astrology or you simply want to explore something new in reading this book, you will likely start to develop a preference one way or another. The preference that is right for you will be entirely dependent upon you, and whatever you choose for yourself will be what is right for you.

As a way to start dipping your feet into the understanding of astrology that you will develop, let's start with taking a look at what astrology looks like around the world. You will see that it varies a lot from Eastern to Western, and Hindu astrology is also different as well. Even then, you will see slight variations within the same form of astrology that you will need to consider as well. So, let's get started! We will first look at astrology itself. And then, we will address the three primary variants that you are likely to encounter.

Remember, you will need to choose the form of astrology that works for you—no one else can do that for you. You have to be able to pick out what it is that you want at any given point in time.

## Reviewing Astrology

Ultimately, all astrology is based upon looking at the stars. Most people tend to refer to astrology as either Western, Eastern, or Vedic. Each of these will have its own divisions, and as you can probably infer from the name, have areas in the world where they are generally preferred.

Each of these forms of astrology will have its own methods of looking at the skies. They will each have their own ways of dividing up the information that they are using, and they will use that information themselves in ways that will be quite beneficial. From being able to see that the traditional Western form is going to revolve around the tropical zodiac to recognizing the Eastern and Hindu preference for the sidereal zodiac, you can see that there are small variations.

Despite these variations, they all work within the same premises: You take the moment of birth or some other important moment, and you then essentially take a snapshot of the sky. You use the exact positions of the stars, the planets, the sun, and the Moon at that moment, and that becomes the chart that determines your life. Some believe that the stars, at that moment, will reveal the karmic balance of your life, writing out what you have done, what you will do, and how you will be rewarded, and how you will suffer. They influence the life that you have, and they tell you exactly what will happen—but you have to know how to read it.

## Eastern Astrology

Now, it is important to note that eastern astrology refers to all astrology that is eastern, including Chinese. That means that you could include Vedic astrology in this scope. However, for the purpose of this chapter, we will separate out Vedic astrology into its own category: Hindu Astrology.

With Eastern astrology, you are looking at forms of astrology that come from the Vedas. They are at least 5000 years old and may even be older. This form of astrology is meant to be much more exact than Western. When you use Eastern or Chinese astrology, you are looking at a form that is slightly different from Hindu Astrology.

Rather than recognizing the idea of fire, water, earth, and air, Eastern astrology focuses on just three—in particular; it follows the three harmonies of Heaven, Earth, and Water. It also recognizes other principles that are slightly different than anything that you would see in other forms, such as the concept of yin and yang.

Eastern Astrology will look at both the Sun and the Moon and will calculate information about a person or events based upon the heavenly stems, the earthly branches, and the lunisolar calendar. That, along with the time calculation, will allow for the individual reading the eastern astrology to understand more.

This form of astrology was pushed primarily in the Zhou dynasty in China, from 1046-256 BC, and grew rapidly. Like Hindu Astrology, it acknowledges just five classical Planets that were visible in the night sky without tools—Mercury, Venus, Mars, Jupiter, and Saturn. Based upon the positions of the planets, the sun, the moon, and any other cosmic bodies, the individual's life and destiny can be discerned. In particular, Jupiter became important and brought about the 12-year cycle that most people think of when they hear the Chinese Zodiac. Chinese Astronomers divided up the celestial circles into 12 and then rounded it up to 12 years, making it not perfectly accurate but close enough to get the point across. Each of these 12 sections represented one of the animals in the Chinese Zodiac.

## Western Astrology

Western astrology is what most Western people are more accustomed to understanding. This is what people reference when they say, "Oh, I'm a Taurus," or "Oh, don't mind me; that's just my Gemini nature speaking!" They are referencing their sign in the Western zodiac. One of the first things that you will need to remember is that the Western zodiac does not perfectly translate to either Eastern or Hindu astrology. There are differences, and whatever your sign is in Western astrology may not actually be your sign in Hindu.

This form focuses on the Sun more than the Moon and then allows you to understand more about who you are as a person. Western astrology becomes important when looking at people in order to get readings on their mental states. However, that doesn't mean that it is worthless or you should forget about it—this form of astrology can be highly useful as well if you look at it and understand the people around you.

## Hindu Astrology

Finally, when you take a look at Hindu, or Vedic, astrology, you are looking at the form that is going to be emphasized in this book. In Vedic astrology, you will be working with a square chart rather than the circular chart that you would see in Western forms of astrology. In addition to this, you will see that you are focusing much more on the Moon rather than the sun, creating an important difference. By focusing more on the moon, you are considering more about what will be in the world around you and what your destiny is assigning you at birth. You will be able to see all sorts of important information that will help you to accurately understand those in your life.

Remember that one of the most important distinctions between the two forms of astrology is the difference between Tropical and Sidereal zodiacs. The Western astrologers turn to tropical zodiacs. This is not quite as exact, and you will see a slightly different starting point. It also means that the two do not line up perfectly. You may be an Aries in one, but not in the other. This is primarily thanks to the different dates and the fact that Vedic astrology accounts for the shifts of the equator that Western astrology does not.

Ultimately, this is the more accurate form of astrology that will help you to get more specific readings. This particular form is going to help you immensely with being able to navigate through everything and ensuring that you can and will be able to be informed about what may be coming.

Manjula Tara

# Chapter 2: An Introduction to the Vedas

The Vedas are the earliest record we have of Indo-Aryan civilization. These books, the most sacred in all of India, are scriptures of the original Hindu religious and spiritual teachings that were said to encompass all life. They have endured the test of time and continue to be seen as the highest form of authority on religion in every aspect of Hinduism. They are recognized and respected by those in India and valued deeply. The word itself, "Veda," translates to wisdom or knowledge. It is believed to be the manifestation of what the Gods have said to the humans. These laws have continued to have an immense influence on the culture and customs of the Hindus and create obligatory duties based on Vedic rituals.

Birth, death, marriage, and just about everything else is believed to be guided by the Vedic texts. The Vedas are known for providing this information to all involved, giving them the ability to understand how to behave and when to do so. The philosophical teachings of the Vedas are used regularly to guide Hindu people in everything that they choose to do.

Being able to understand the Vedas helps you to begin understanding the position taken when reading the stars as well. By understanding what is happening with the Vedas, you start to see that there is a very real opportunity for being able to read and understand other aspects of reading birth charts. For this reason, we are taking the time to delve into the Vedas. By understanding the teachings, what is emphasized and what is not, and more, you will start to get that solid understanding of what is valued and emphasized in astrology as well.

## Revisiting the Vedas

It is hard for anyone to state when the earliest Vedas came from. However, it is believed that they are some of the earliest produced written documents produced by humanity. It was originally passed through verbally, and because it was not written when it was first coined, it is impossible to know exactly when the Vedas was created. However, it is believed that it may date back as far as the late Bronze age—early 1700 BCE.

According to the Vedas and to tradition, humans did not write the Vedas. They were taught via Vedic hymns to the sages, who then passed them down by mouth. They were orally passed on from generation to generation. The formal documentation, however, was done by Vyasa Krishna Dwaipayana around the time of Lord Krishna, 1500 BC.

Within the Vedas, there are four volumes. These are the Rig-Veda, the Sama Veda, the Yajur Veda, and the Atharva Veda. The Rig Veda is the foundation of the text, and the others serve as support for it. Collectively, all four are known as Chathurveda. They are structured the same way for each of the four. There are first the Samhitas, then the Brahmanas, followed by the Aranyakas, and finally, the Upanishads. Each of these provides information and rituals to the people.

## Samhitas

The Samhitas are the hymns and mantras. They are known to be the most ancient form of the Vedas, and within them, there are several different mantras, prayers, hymns, and litanies. These are the oral details in written form. They come from the understanding of "sam," meaning together, and "hita," meaning to put. As such, they are arranged and placed together. They essentially help to bring people to the moment and focus.

## Brahmanas

The Brahmanas are attached to the Samhitas. They are the second layer of text that is included within the Vedas. They exist to explain and instruct the Brahmins, the priests, teachers, and protectors of spiritual and sacred learning, how to perform rituals. They explore the symbolism of the Samhitas as well. The Brahmana literature is also known to list information about the scientific understanding of the Vedic period, such as astronomy and geometry. They contain some information that is mystical and philosophical as well.

Each Veda has at least one Brahmana, and each Brahmana is typically associated with one Vedic school. There are currently less than 20 in existence, with others believed to be destroyed or lost. The oldest Brahmana is dated to have existed in 900 BCE, while the youngest is believed to be from 700 BCE. They allow for understanding the rituals that occurred, detailing in-depth how to perform and why there is a symbolic emphasis on certain words or actions. They are very exact and require exact accent, speed, and pitch, paired with certain movements. They must be perfect. According to Satapatha Brahamana, verbal perfection was necessary to create power for the mantras. However, without that perfection, with just one simple mistake, everything could come crashing down. If there were mistakes during rituals, it was believed that the ritual would be entirely powerless.

## Aranyakas

The Aranyakas are the philosophies that exist beyond the rituals and texts. They are the second to last part of the Vedas and provide information discussing the perspectives of those rituals. They may, at times, discuss what it is that is meant by the ritual. Other times, they may also show information about the symbolism.

## Upanishads

The Upanishads exist as the end of the Vedas. They are a sort of last words of the texts. Translated, the meaning of "Upanishad" is "sit down closely." Like a student would understand the information that was intended for that individual, the Upanishads call upon you to listen closely and illustrate ways to understand the more difficult or obscure concepts and passages that are embedded within the Vegas.

These are the most recent of the writings of the Vedas and are there to provide us with the information that we are missing. They help you to understand the concepts of Brahman and Atman. They encourage you to build up the foundation necessary to practice and live according to the Vedas.

## The Rig-Veda

The Rig Veda is translated as "knowledge of the verses [mantras]." This is the most prominent of the four Vedas and is the first one written. It is built up with 1028 hymns, which are dedicated to several gods and deities. The hymns contain ten books, known as mandalas or circles. The older books had hymns that focused on the gods and goddesses, while younger books found focus on philosophical material such as virtues, society, and general metaphysical issues. The hymns found in the Rig Veda included praises, blessings, and even sacrifices. They are written in such a way as poetry, and when chanting the words out loud, it is believed that you are able to achieve a state of relaxation and meditation.

In the Rig Veda, the most prominent deity is Agni, the god of fire. Also addressed in this book include Indra, Varuna, Mitra, the Ashvis, and the Maruts.

The emphasis in the Rig Veda is the focus on religious observance, practicing it correctly. It is based upon the concept of universal vibrations that were understood by the sages that first heard them. They also address some very fundamental questions that help address the concept of existence. They emphasize the idea that Hinduism reiterates—that life exists solely to prepare us for union with the Divine.

## The Sama Veda

The Sama Veda translates to the knowledge of the melodies (saman). The hymns found in the Sama Veda come from the Rig Veda and do not teach their own lessons. However, they are recognized nonetheless. They are the meanings of the songs that are found in the Rig Veda. As explained, the Rig Veda is like the word, and the Sama Veda is like the inherent meaning of that word.

## The Yajur Veda

The Yajur Veda is a collection that is meant to provide ceremonial religion. It is the ability to understand the sacrificial acts, prayers, and movements that must occur together. They work well together and provide the individual with the opportunity to understand the rituals of the Rig Veda. There are six complete recessions of the Yajur Veda that provide that understanding.

## The Atharva Veda

The Atharva Veda is the knowledge of the Spells. This one is where there is differing information. The Rig Veda creates the foundation, and the Sama and Yajur Vedas build upon the Rig Veda, using the information within it. The Atharva Veda, on the other hand, creates new information, teachings, and prayers. It is the second most important of the Vedas and allows individuals to start learning more. The hymns include more key players than the Rig Veda ad. They are also typically a bit simpler in their language that is used. They are able to provide more diversity as a result. However, due to the divergence between the Rig Veda and the Atharva Veda, there are scholars who choose not to include it as a Veda text at all.

This book is filled with spells that are meant to ward off danger and spirits, as well as chats, prayers, hymns, rituals, marriage, and funeral ceremonies. It is believed to be derived from the priest known as Atharvan, who was a healer and an innovator. Though it is not likely that Atharvan himself composed these works, it is believed to be related to him. It is comprised of 20 books of 730 hymns, some of which refer to the Rig Veda as well.

Like the other texts, the Aranyakas, Brahmanas, Samhitas, and Upanishads present themselves within this text as well.

## Sruti vs. Smriti

One thing that must be touched upon is that knowledge in the Vedas is divided into two categories. There is sruti knowledge and smriti knowledge. Each has a different source to reference. Sruti is that which is heard—it is the knowledge that you gain through authorities. In the case of Hinduism, it is the authority of the Divine passed into the Vedas. It is stated that the Vedas are Sruit—that they are passed on from the Divine to the sages that were able to translate them to pass them on to the others in the religion. It is supposed to be the knowledge that was not created by the sages, but rather, they interpreted the meaning of the messages from the Gods.

Sruti is absolute—it is to be obeyed without being questioned. To question it is to question the Gods themselves, and they have knowledge of the divine plan. They know what they are doing. They know what the Universe has in store. They are able to guide us if we are willing to listen to what is said. This is why it is so important to listen to and adhere to the teachings of the Vedas.

Smirti knowledge is that which is remembered—it is the knowledge that comes from other texts. It is information that can be directly attributed to a human author. The Vedas are believed to be authorless, transmitted verbally for years. However, Smirti knowledge can be directly attributed to one individual.

Smirti literature includes the teachings surrounding the Vedas that are known to be written by people. It is the six Vedangas, the epics, the Dharmasutras and Dharmasastras, the Arthasasastras, the Puranas, the Kavya, and more. The Smirti texts exist in several different versions with different translations and readings. They are fluid and can be rewritten by others without much issue.

The Smirti texts still include very heavy sway on the people, but they are not believed to have the same degree of authority that the others do. They tend to influence the laws.

Because the Sruti texts are divine and the smriti are human in origin, it is believed that the Sruti is absolute. There is no rewriting them—they are to be translated and written down exactly as they are, word for word.

## The Teachings of the Vedas

The Vedas are there to teach you how you can and will be able to understand how to live. They mean to teach you the knowledge, and the knowledge that you accept from the Vedas is meant to enlighten you. It is believed that your mind and soul are conditioned. The conditioned souls are defects, and those defects prevent you from achieving liberation. There are four key defects in the conditioned souls that must be corrected, and until they are corrected, the individual will not be liberated.

The first defect is that of making mistakes. The mistakes that individuals make can cause them problems.

The second defect is to be illusioned, related to the idea of seeing things as something that they are not. This is referred to as Maya—that which is not. Everyone accepts that their bodies are themselves. They believe that they are created from their corporeal form. If someone asks you who you are, you probably state that you are a certain person. You insist that you are a few characteristics that fall under the person that you are. However, that is Maya—you are discussing the body. However, you are more than the body. You are your soul, and your soul is on a constant journey to achieve enlightenment—to achieve that joining with the divine.

The third defect is that of cheating. We all have the ability to cheat, but not everyone does it. There are many who choose to live honest lives without allowing their propensity to cheat to impact them. They live stating that they can be their own people, and they are, sometimes. However, they may also present themselves as what they think they are, even though they are not that person.

Finally, the last flaw is that we are not perfect. Our senses are imperfect as well. We may rely on them to be accurate, but remember this—your senses can be betrayed. They can be altered. They can cause all sorts of issues for you if you don't understand that they are imperfect.

Those who live by the Vedas are known as Varnasrama. They are those who accept this idea that they are inherently flawed. They recognize that there are eight divisions of varna and ashrama.

These are the four divisions of society and the four divisions of spiritual life. The divisions of society are known as Brahmana, Kshatriya, vaisya, and sudra.

Brahmana refers to intelligent men who understand what Brahman is. The Kshatriyas refer to the administrators. They are the ones who are able to keep up with the information that they need. The third group is the vaisya and is the mercantile. They are everywhere, and these natural classifications can be found everywhere. Sudra refers to the worker class—those who are likely to do tasks that are typically thought of as menial.

The Vedic principles, such as the above, are accepted as true and cannot be false. They must be accepted. Remember, the Vedas themselves are not human knowledge—they are from the divine. The Vedic knowledge is known as sruti—that which is heard. It is not experiential. It is like the knowledge gained from parents. As a child, you simply accept what your parents have to say as true because you trust that they know better than you. The knowledge that you gain from them comes because you accept their word. Likewise, the word in the Rig Veda comes from the Divine. It is accepted in the same manner.

# Chapter 3: Vedic Teachings in the Modern World

Despite how old the Vedas are, they are still an integral part of Indian and Hindu teachings. It was once taught to others through a systematic manner that was meant to teach the individuals how to live. It was to show one how to accept and meet their responsibilities and also made it clear that the individuals had strict duties that had to be met. Nowadays, the teachings are a bit different, but they are still prevalent throughout the nation.

Education is designed to teach us how to exist. If you think about it, we all go to school primarily because we are being shaped and molded into the people that society needs us to be. We are driven to create these versions of ourselves, being sculpted by the structure of education. Especially in the Western world, the education system has sort of surrounded itself around the concept of creating more workers. The children are taught to recite and follow directions rather than emphasizing critical thinking. This is a carryover from the Industrial Revolution and the intense need for people who would simply follow the law at all costs. It is meant to provide a sort of understanding of what the world would need.

Likewise, the Vedic teachings do the same. As children are taught the Vedas, they learn over time. They develop a solid understanding of the people that they need to be. The teachings of the Vedas are tied into the schooling itself. And, as individuals are educated more and more, they start understanding more about the Vedas and the information that they need to know.

Nowadays, most Vedic knowledge is taught in universities as a part of the religion departments. This approach is not fair to the Vedic knowledge in the first place. By teaching the Vedas as another branch of the department of religion instead of as its own individual topic, there can be major repercussions. This can be highly problematic for the individual and can lead to all sorts of issues. The problem with this approach is that Vedic knowledge is not just limited to that of religion. It is the approach to all areas in life. The Vedas emphasize everything, from religion to civics. They provide us with a way of interpreting the world and seeing that there are certain fundamental foundations that branch out, much like a tree, to encompass all kinds of knowledge, not just religion.

Everything in the material world is just ideas. We can understand the ideas, but we do not understand why they are there in the first place, and this is problematic. The problem with this is that education should be focused on developing an understanding of how the entirety of it was produced.

The key to understanding Vedic texts is to recognize that they have two layers of knowledge. There is primary knowledge and secondary knowledge. The Vedic texts do teach how the universe was created. It is stated that Lord Brahma was created first and is the very first person to undergo education before applying that information into the creation of anything else. The primary creation was the creation of the universal principles that will constantly apply, no matter where. Then, the secondary creation principles refer to the applications of universal principles.

It is believed that Lord Brahma is the topmost principle—the very first principle. He is represented on a lotus. He understands the universe from the top down, with the top being the space and down the stem being everything else. He attempts to understand the universe in this matter, but he never finds the bottom of the universe.

This is because the act of climbing down is a metaphor—it is the metaphorical understanding that you can endlessly look deeper and deeper into something but still have questions. Think about it—we have the universe. Smaller than the universe, we have galaxies. The galaxies have solar systems. The solar systems have planets. Earth has continents. The continents have countries. The countries have cities. The cities have neighborhoods. The neighborhoods have households. The households have families. The families have people. The people are built up of biological components. The components are composed of elements, which are composed of atoms. You can continually go deeper. You can keep asking, "well, what is smaller than that? What makes that possible?" By continuing to ask this question and continuing to go deeper and deeper, you continue to learn and explore more information.

Likewise, Brahma realized that trying to go from the top down was not going to help him. The deeper and deeper you go, the smaller you get and the more specific you get, but there is never that foundation found. Just as you can divide the number 1 indefinitely without ever reaching true 0, you can continually go down further and further in attempting to understand something.

The lesson learned is that you must go up. Instead of looking at the smallest matter as the foundation of something, we must see the biggest picture as the foundation and work backward. This brings us to the idea of everything and nothing. Everything is at the top of the universe, while there is nothing at the bottom.

Lord Brahma learned this in his own education. He had to learn that starting at the bottom is impossible—we must build from the top down. He took this information and began to use it to create more. He was the secondary creator, the one who created everything else from those principles of information.

This ought to be the child's education as well. In the modern-day, we get so caught up with trying to get to the bottom of something, to know why something works the way that it does, and why that works the way it does in an endless cycle of trying to delve deeper and deeper into the information. However, this does us no favors. Like Lord Brahma, knowledge ought to be taught to allow individuals to look down. They should start at the biggest picture as the foundation for their knowledge and work off of it. We should begin with this idea of everything and slowly bring it down to nothing as a result. The more that we do this and the more detailed that we get, the more the child learns.

All things have these two extremes. We have science, and then we have molecular biology as the tip of one branch, and even then, there would be divisions from there as well.

Modern Vedic knowledge is believed to be developed little by little. It comes in ten different stages that all build upon each other to create that solid foundation that will guide the child through their life.

The first stage is the concept of sensing objects. You can sense objects around you. You can see the flowers growing on the ground. You can see your friend standing next to you or the door in front of you. Additionally, you understand that there is the concept of change. You can pick the flower, and the flower will no longer be growing on the ground. You can open the door to move to another room. You can eat the banana on the table, and it disappears. Time changes the world around you, and you can see that as well. It also brings about the idea that there is pain and pleasure as well.

The second stage is that of properties. You recognize that there are colors and shapes, and we can point out things that are those colors or shapes, but we cannot convey the idea of that color. You know that you have green, and you can identify it as green, but you cannot explain the concept of green without simply saying it is green. These are fixed properties, and you can do so with shapes as well. It is round because all sides are round—they don't have edges.

The third stage is understanding that there are several different types of senses. It understands that the individual can sense things with various different senses, and likewise, other people can sense things with various senses as well. For example, you can see that ball on the floor, and so can the person next to you. This stage brings about it understanding that other people get that same degree of perception.

The fourth stage brings about the understanding that there are some concepts that apply to several things. For example, you may have one flower, or there are dozens of them. All flowers are flowers, just like the one in your hand. And, there can be flowers that look completely different that are still just flowers. This represents the start of understanding beyond just the physical, sensual experience in the world.

The fifth stage is that in which we start understanding the diversity of concepts that we know actually stem from a few root concepts. We start seeing the beginning of thinking diversely. We see that there are all sorts of animals, but they can all be classified scientifically. We understand that there are dozens of different vegetables and fruits, but they are all plants. We understand that things are alive, or they are not based upon a concept, or that some things sink while others float. We start to see that there are just a few essential concepts and ideas that create a broad theory that becomes more and more diverse; the further it gets from the one root idea.

The sixth state involves the child developing an understanding that all theories that we have been motivated by our desire to begin to understand. We have goals that lead us to start deconstructing concepts, or we have problems that need to be solved, and deconstructing the ideas grants that understanding as well. The further that we go into this, the more information that we get and the better we become at understanding the world around us. We understand that sometimes we have conflicting ideas, and those conflicting ideas stem from the fact that we have conflicting goals that we are trying to achieve.

The seventh step involves the child realizing that conflicts cannot be resolved without some degree of moral principles of right and wrong. If we don't have right and wrong, how do you know which principle is the right one? We have to have this concept to help ourselves better understand what we are seeing and doing. These ideas of right and wrong, then, must also be applied by society at large, and we must all share moral principles that help us to navigate through the world that we have.

The eighth step of learning brings with it the understanding that even though we have moral principles, not everyone follows them. Not everyone is willing to play by the rules. And, when there are people who do not play by the rules, there must be consequences as well. After all, there are consequences to all actions—we don't live in a vacuum. This opens the door to an understanding of karma and transmigration through reincarnation.

The ninth step involves the understanding of transmigration. When we see that there is this concept of transmigration, we gain the understanding that there are other animals and living beings as well who have their own sensations and perceptions just like people do. They, too, have the capacity to perceive the world around them and interact with it. However, what they lack in their ability to understand it. They do not understand how they got into the life that they live. They are simply there, in the present.

Finally, the tenth stage involves the child recognizing that humans can see this concept of repeated birth and death and that this is the problem with life. The whole purpose of life is to find a way to exit the cycle of rebirth once and for all. The purpose of life is the need for escaping and transcending the need to live. Life is suffering. It may be beautiful at times, but it is painful. We suffer. We come into the world painfully and suddenly, and we often leave the world painfully as well. This is the cycle of life and rebirth, but the soul will not remember past lives. The soul repeats this cycle over and over until it is finally able to escape it.

It is essential for modern children to go through schooling to learn to see the world in this way. However, there is a noted lack of this these days, leading to children who are lost. It leads to children who have no idea what the goal is for them after school. They have no understanding of what they should be doing and how to get to the end goal.

Nowadays, the modern method of teaching Vedic education happens much like how it did once before. It involves the creation of what is known as the Gurukul. This is a school-type setting in which the gurus live alongside their teachers for years, learning from the teacher, and respecting the information that is learned. There has been a resurgence of Gurukul education in India in particular, designed to allow for individuals to reclaim their culture and heritage, encouraged further by the fact that parents, academics, and even the government, encourages it.

In this setting, there is a simplicity to life. They adhere to a strict schedule and respect their teachers. However, despite the fact that there are several children under the care of their guru, it is actually the case that equality and independence are pushed. The children are equal to the guru, and they are guided through prayer, meditation, yoga, and learning how to be adults. They learn more about the world and also develop into positive influences on the society that they are going to live in as adults.

This is not the same as religious education—it is the teaching of being a well-rounded individual. There is an emphasis on a few key principles by the gurus in these settings.

One of the most important concepts to consider is personality development. In Vedic education, the goal is to develop the personality through developing self-respect and self-realization. Through getting to know oneself deeply, good judgment can be developed as well. Daily tasks that focus on physical, mental, and emotional development matter. The students tend to build their personalities based upon this as well, and they discover a degree of multidimensionality to themselves as well. They become well-adjusted, resilient, and ready to contribute to the world.

They also create a form of character as well. Morality must go alongside the depth of knowledge that is learned. When you learn separately from developing morality, you can have all sorts of issues that make it almost pointless. Students had to run on strict schedules. They were expected to remain celibate and had to forsake luxuries and comforts to help them develop that morality. They were expected to be good simply because being good is the moral choice that ought to be honored. They were taught to be these individuals who did not require such needs.

The Gurukuls also pushed for an understanding of both civic and social duties as well. The students were explicitly taught that they had to contribute to society. They lived as equals, regardless of their own social status, and all cleaned and shared the same chores. They were taught that it was their duty to keep their home clean and that outside in the world, they must become good partners, spouses, and parents as well. Their wealth that they accumulated should not be used for themselves, but rather, should be given to society instead, and it should be earned honorably.

Education in these schools is also designed to teach as well. In particular, there is an emphasis on learning out of the experience through practicality. By focusing on this sort of vocational training, the students learn the value of all jobs. There is value in weaving or in pottery, even if those jobs do not always create glamorous lives.

There is also a strong emphasis on developing traditions and culture through the Gurukuls. There is a necessary emphasis on training through cultural traditions and starting to recognize that teaching is not just about rote memorization and knowledge, but also in imparting the traditions to the next generation as well. This means that the students learned that they had three debts that they owed to the world. They owed a debt to the gods, to the past gurus that taught them, and to their ancestors as well. They are taught that they must serve the gods, and in doing so, they have paid the first debt. In learning the teaching of the past intellectuals, they have paid the second debt. Finally, by raising children and educating them in the traditions, they have paid their debt to the ancestors as well.

Finally, they are taught to emphasize enlightenment. Education is meant to make students become productive members of society, and that is further emphasized simply due to the fact that the children are taught to perform the rituals of their culture. There are certain prayers and rituals that must happen daily and also at certain milestones that are important as well. In doing so, there is an emphasis on the spiritual world as well, creating emphasis on achieving enlightenment. The goal is to create people who understand that the material world is maya and that their ultimate goal is not to simply amass everything they can, but rather to grant them the ability to understand what they are doing, so they can eventually achieve that enlightenment. At the end of the day, the current life is such an incredibly slim part of one's whole life, and therefore, the material goods amassed during it are not nearly as important as many of the others.

# Chapter 4: The Vedas and Vedic Astrology

There is more to the Vedas than just teaching people to be good and kind. There is actually information that is directly related to Vedic astrology within them. By reading through them, you start to see the influence of the Vedas on how the charts in Vedic astrology are read. The knowledge actually predates the information that came from Babylonia and Greece, and it is possible to see very clear references in the Rig Veda that directly apply to the reading of Vedic charts as well.

For example, the number 360 is incredibly important. This number represents the number of degrees in a circle. In the Rig Veda, there are direct references to a chakra or wheel with 360 spokes in the sky. Additionally, there are clear references to numbers such as 12, 24, 36, 48, and other such related numbers that commonly occur in Vedic symbolism, and they are also prevalent in Vedic astrology.

Thanks to the name, it becomes quite clear that there is absolutely supposed to be a connection between the Vedas and Vedic astrology. However, understanding the references will also provide some clarity to what you will need to know about the charts that you will eventually be reading as well.

Jyotisa is actually one of the Vedanga—the six auxiliary disciplines that are used in support of Vedic rituals. Keep in mind that Jyotisa and all of the Vedanga are Smirti—they are believed to be influenced by the word of the Divine without actually being the word of the Divine. They draw from the Divine's word and the Sruti Rig Veda by using the teachings to further understand. The Rig Veda is like a springing board for the ideas—the foundation is there, but they are able to achieve newer, greater heights because of the fact that they know what they are doing. This is essential to understand. It effectively means that the roots of Vedic astrology as we know it are found in the Rig Veda. They are taken from and extrapolated upon to create the understandings that we see today.

We can see this throughout the texts. We can see hymns in which it is said that there are five characters that are representative of the Planets, or there are groups of three that represent the Earth, the Air, and the Heavens. There are all sorts of references that clearly help with the division of the Planets and signs as we know them to create our understanding of Astrology in general.

The hymns of Dirghatamas clearly identify a zodiac of 360 degrees, dividing it in several ways, including by and 12. Why is this relevant, you may ask? Simple: We have twelve signs that play a role in reading the zodiac. These are Aries, Taurus, Gemini, Cancer, Leo, Virgo, Libra, Scorpio, Sagittarius, Capricorn, Aquarius, and Pisces. We have twelve signs and twelve houses in our natal charts as well. Each sign gets 30 degrees in the sky.

In Vedic astrology, the main God is the Sun God, known as Vishnu. He rules over the heavens and is identified as a pole star in the sky. This is the central point that controls the motions and creates the skies that we see.

In the Rig Veda l.155.6, it is said, "With four times ninety names, he sets in motion moving forces like a turning wheel." This is a direct reference to Vishnu and his forms and names—there is one for each degree of the zodiac. The reason for the division of four is likely to relate to the seasons being divided as well. We have the solstices and the equinoxes.

Further in the Rig Veda, it is stated, "Seven half embryos form the seed of the world. They stand in the dharma by the direction of Vishnu." It is believed that this may be a reference to the seven Planets that are relevant in Vedic astrology.

In Hymn I.164, you also see a very clear description of the Zodiac as well: "Of this adorable old invoker is a middle brother who is pervasive. He has a third brother, whose back carries ghee. There I saw the Lord of the people who has seven children."

This can be broken down into a few different parts that directly correlate to the Zodiac. First, there is an understanding of the three Gods. There is the Fire on Earth, the Wind in the skies, and the Sun in heaven. The Sun is believed to have seven children—the Sun, the Moon, and the five Planets we look to in order to see our fates in the stars: Mercury, Venus, Mars, Jupiter, and Saturn.

The division of three also appears again in understanding the various elements. Each element appears in the Planets three times in three different forms—these are the mutable, fixed, and cardinal influences on the elements, which the Zodiac are divided by. Aries, for example, is the cardinal fire sign ruled by Mars. Leo is the fixed fire sign ruled by the Sun. Finally, Sagittarius is the mutable fire sign ruled by Jupiter. They are all fiery, and yet, they have their own divisions and classifications. These divisions directly relate to the divisions of space as well. Cardinal signs are born of the Earth. Fixed signs are ruled by the Heavens. The mutable signs are ruled by the atmosphere.

Continuing in the hymn from above, we get: "Seven yokes the chariot that has a single wheel. One horse that has seven names carries it. The wheel has three naves, is undecaying and never overcomes, where all these beings are placed."

This is further describing the Zodiac—the Zodiac is a single line of constellations in the skies that circles the Earth. The seven Planets are all forms of the Sun, and the horse is the symbol of energy and force.

The hymn continues to the next verse: "This chariot which the seven have mounted has seven wheels and is carried by seven horses. The seven sisters sing forth together, where are hidden the seven names of the cows."

This is relevant, as well. The seven Planets create their seven rotations around the Earth at different speeds. They all have their own energies. They each carry their own powers and have their own names. They are the influences that are created by the Planets that we refer to when we look at the Zodiac and their power over us.

"The wheel of law with twelve spokes does not decay as it revolves around heaven. Oh Fire, here your 720 sons abide."

The Zodiac has twelve signs within it. There are 720 divisions if you divide each degree into twins, creating a total of 360.

"The Father with five feet and twelve forms, they say, dwells in the higher half of heaven full of waters. Others say that he is the clear-seeing one who dwells below in a sevenfold wheel that has six spokes."

The five feet of the father reference the planets, or the five elements associated with the five sensory organs of humans. The twelve forms reference the zodiac signs. The Sun in the higher half of heaven with water is the sign of Leo in Cancer.

Beyond just that hymn that has been quoted, there is more to it as well. The Creator is said to have created the stars, assigning an animal to each. There were initially five animals that were assigned to the constellations. The animals that were assigned include the man, goat, ram, bull, and horse. These are all Zodiac animals as well.

## The Vedas and Vedic Astrology

The roots of Vedic astrology run deep in the Vedas and eventually were used to create the form of astronomy that we know today. The modern form of Vedic astrology that we know today was actually formed out of "Jyotish," the science of light in the Vedas. Like most forms of ancient knowledge, this was traditionally taught through oral transmission. This means that the earliest forms of it are not present for us to see—we must go off of what is currently recorded by the people. The term Vedic astrology, or what we call Vedic astrology, was not coined until the early 1980s, making it quite modern. Prior to that, in the early 19th century, it was known as Hindu astrology.

Nevertheless, even if Vedic astrology was not in the Vedas, it still draws heavily from the teachings within it. After all, the very Vedic astrology that we all turn to is actually just the manifestation of the movements of the Planets and the stars in the sky.

This is further evidenced in the fact that Vedic scholars had very complex math at the time. They already worked with the concept of zero, the 10-based counting method, and algebra and algorithm. The first time that such math came to be recorded was actually in the history of the Vedas. It is potentially the case that the Indians actually had these concepts before the Greeks, who are commonly credited. This is likely due to the fact that India could have referenced Greece rather than the other way around.

Why would they have needed such complex math? This is a question that is hard to answer, but it is also utilized in the creation of astrological charts. Through math, it was possible to cast the natal charts that would allow for the individuals in question to know about their lives. They could get guidance from being able to calculate the exact positions of the Planets in the sky and then interpret them to determine something that mattered.

As we have mentioned, Vedic astrology is significantly more accurate than the traditional form of Western astrology, and in part, this is due to the fact that they were so much more exact with how they calculated out their placements. They acknowledged that the people in the world were born at a certain moment for a certain reason, and the stars and planets in the sky at that very moment of birth was telling of the karma that those individuals carried. However, it was not as simple as typing in one's birth location and time to an algorithm runner online- they would have to calculate things out by hand, running the math and being as accurate as possible.

Today, you are much luckier—you can simply go online and web search "Vedic astrology birth chart calculator." This saves you plenty of math and time—all of which is complex and requires too many variables to do clearly and easily. Remember, the chart is based upon the sky at the moment of your birth from where you are from. The sky at 7:32 PM on January 7, 1992, in Seattle, Washington, is going to look significantly different than the sky at 7:32 PM on January 7, 1992, in Amsterdam or in Tokyo or Dubai. The sky varies from location to location enough to mean that you must consider the influence that location would have on your chart.

Nevertheless, Vedic astrologers were able to calculate it out. They were able to take a person, a location, and a date and time and start calculating out the positions of all of the stars and planets at that moment so their signs could be placed.

# Chapter 5: Historical Figures in Vedic Astrology

As with any rich history, there are all sorts of people that are attributed to the success and thriving of Vedic astrology. Being able to understand the key players and influencers who not only passed down Vedic astrology knowledge but also recorded, studied, and enhanced it, helps you to see the timeline and the amount of history that goes into the readings that you are creating.

Within this chapter, we are only addressing a few of the key figures and locations in Vedic astrology, but they matter immensely. Being able to see these key figures matters and will help you with being able to understand more about what you are understanding. It may also aid in helping you to gain a deeper appreciation, especially as you are able to utilize all of the knowledge of humanity in your hands. Within seconds, you can enter the date, time, and location of your birth and have a perfect picture of the sky. You can even use calculators to give you a complete natal chart in moments just by virtue of flashing it in front of you.

When you follow through with this particular craft, you are learning more and more about the world around you. You are learning to recognize and honor people who cultivated the path that you are following and who made Jyotish into what it is today. This is a great way to connect to the past and to gain that understanding and respect for the people of the past who deserve it.

We are taking a look at a few of the most influential figures here—these are people who usually coined books that became critical to understanding the world around them. They are people who are capable of seeing the world for what it could be. Let's take the time to give each of these people some respect for the influence that they had over the world and over this science, beginning with the one typically credited as creating the first of the Vedic texts.

## Parasara Muni

Parasara was a maharishi—a member of the highest order of the ancient sages. He was well-versed in understanding nature, the world around him, and applying the science from the Vedas to the world around him. He is known as the author of many of the ancient Indian texts that are tied to the Vedas as well. He is specifically believed to be the author of the first Purana—the Vishnu Purana. It was eventually rewritten by his son. However, throughout the Vishnu Purana, there are several references to Parasara as the author.

According to legend, Sage Parasara was raised by his grandfather, the great Vasishtha, because his father had been consumed by an angry demon who had once been a king. The demon is said to have devoured him in anger. As a result, Parasara is said to have attempted a ritual sacrifice to destroy the demons, and many were destroyed. However, his grandfather told him that "Anger is the passion of fools; it becometh not a wise man... Anger... is the destruction of all that man obtains by arduous exertions of fame and of devout austerities. ... Mercy is the might of the righteous." In convincing him not to continue his onslaught of demons, Parasara let go of his rage over his father's death.

Legend has it that Sage Parasara was traveling across the country and one night, stopped on the banks of the river Ganga. He was allowed to stay in the house of the village chief. At dawn, the chief's daughter, Satyavati, was asked to take Parasara to his next destination. On the ferry, however, Parasara could smell the stench of raw fish, despite the fact that there were no fish within the river.

When he asked where the smell was coming from, he discovered that Satyavati was actually the daughter of a fisherman who had pursued the same occupation. She was the one who smelled. He called her "Matsyagandha," meaning the one who smells of fish. She was ashamed and Parasara, feeling sorry for his cruel taunting, gave her the boon of fine fragrance.

He found himself quite attracted to her and wanted to be with her intimately. However, she was afraid to do so due to the crowds of people on either side of the river. So, using his own mystic powers, he created a dense sheet of mist around an island. They soon had a son named Vyasa. However, she did not appreciate his travels. They separated, and in parting, he granted her a boon for her lost virginity.

## Vyasa

Vyasa is the son of Parasara and Satyavati. He is believed to have written the Puranas and the *Mahabharata*. He is also believed to be the traditional compiler of the Vedas as well. In particular, the Guru Purnima is dedicated to him as well. It is known as the Vyasa Purnima and is believed to be the day he was born as well as the day he divided the Vedas. He is believed to be one of the seven Chiranjivis (immortals), and according to legend, he still lives today.

According to legend, when Parasara left Satyavati, he also took Vyasa with him, leaving her to move on, with her virginity restored, and she eventually married Shantanu. Together, Satyavati and Shantanu had two sons, named Chitrangada and Vichitravirya. However, neither of them had an heir before they both died young. Despite this, Vichitravirya, at the time of his death, had two wives, Ambika and Ambalika. When Satyavati was eventually left widowed, she asked her stepson, Bhishma, to marry the queens,

Ambika and Ambalika. However, he denied the request, reminding her that he had taken a vow of celibacy. Satyavati then mentioned that she had a secret son and asked for him to bring home Yvasa to impregnate both widows, following a tradition known as Niyoga, in which a man is chosen to impregnate a widowed woman who is childless.

At this point in time, Vyasa had already compiled the Vedas. He was quite ugly, with matted hair and a dark skin tone. Upon seeing him, Ambika was frightened. She closed her eyes. However, as a result, their child was born blind. Ambalika turned pale when she first saw Vyasa, and as a result, her child was also born pale. Satyavati asked for Vyasa to impregnate Ambika once more to try to have another son that was not blind. However, she sent her maid instead. The maid remained calm and had a child as well.

Vyasa is believed to have split the Vedas, gaining the name Veda Vyasa, or Vyasa Veda. He is believed to have done so to allow for the knowledge provided to be better and easier understood by the people.

## Lagadha

Lagadha is one of the oldest known Hindu mathematicians and astronomers and is known to have written the Vedanga Jyotisha. This is written in two parts—the Rik and Yajur recensions. The first part is composed of 36 verses in Sanskrit that address eclipses, a lunar calendar, and calculating out time. Within the Vedanga Jyotisha, the lunar and solar eclipses can also be calculated out. The lunar month begins on a New Moon day and one lunar month lasts for 29.5 days. One year is 12 lunar months and is roughly 354 days long.

This has had a huge mark on astrology—it paved the way for understanding the movements of the heavens and how it worked.

He was able to mark each lunar month into 30 equal parts, known as tithi. His contributions allowed him to create the arithmetic necessary to calculate repeating astronomical events.

Other than the information that is in the Vedanga Jyotisha being attributed to him, very little is known about his personal life. However, the Vedanga Jyotisha is still one of the most influential and important texts in Vedic astrology.

## Yavanesvara

Yavanesvara was a man who wrote the *Yavanajataka*—the "Sayings of the Greeks." His name translates to the Lord of the Greeks. He is said to have translated the Greek language into his own, allowing for much of the information to be translated into Sanskrit. He was a Greek who had come to live in India and was able to understand the information. Through understanding the languages, he was able to allow for the comparisons of the Zodiac signs, the understandings of the sky, and more.

The *Yavanajataka* is one of the oldest texts of Indian astrology as a result. He came to be capable of providing much to the Indian understanding of history, and the information has been shared both ways. However, there was more to it than simply creating a direct translation—he actually translated it so that contextually, they were comparable as well. He was able to begin creating the right context. Instead of giving Greek gods who were naturally in the Greek astrology and astronomy, he included a translation directly into Hindu gods as well. He changed the context to make sure that the understanding of the Greek astrology would actually be relevant to those who were reading the translations. He also worked in the Indian caste system as well to ensure that people could better understand it. He also included the Greek explanation for the Babylonian theory of the motions of the planets. It was written in Sanskrit prose. However, it no longer exists.

This was very much of that point in which both forms of astrology came together. He strongly influenced astrology as well. The understanding with the Vedic and Hindu figures helped propel his work into popularity, and he even managed to separate astrology and astronomy with his work as well. Up until that point, they had been one concept.

## Brahmagupta

Brahmagupta was an Indian mathematician and astronomer. He wrote two important texts in his lifetime in both math and astronomy. In particular, he wrote the Brahmasphuta Siddhanta, translated to the "Correctly established doctrine of Brahma." He was the first one to begin computing with 0, allowing for all sorts of additional math to be completed. Though he is now a very influential figure, at the time, he faced great criticism from other astronomers.

In particular, some of his most important contributions were incredibly important. They included the calculations of the position of heavenly bodies over time. He was able to also calculate out rising and setting times, conjunctions, and solar and lunar eclipses. As you can imagine, his math was highly important to the theories and applications that mattered.

He also rejected the idea that the Moon was further from the Sun, backing up his understanding as well. He explained this by asking how would waxing and waning of the Moon be able to be calculated by the longitude of the Moon? If the Moon were above the Sun, it would always be bright. Likewise, he pointed out that the brightness would always be in the direction of the Sun as well.

# Aryabhata

Aryabhata was one of the first major mathematician astronomers from India. He also wrote the Aryabhatiya and the Arya Siddhanta. These two texts are loaded with the information that he had studied. He correctly stated that Earth spins upon its access each day and that the movement of the stars is relative thanks to the motion caused by the rotation of the earth rather than anything else. He states this in the first chapter of the Aryabhatiya. He insisted on a geocentric model of the solar system, stating that the Sun and Moon were both carried by epicycles that both revolved around the Earth. While this was not entirely correct, it did begin the understanding of the Planets.

He was also able to explain eclipses, both solar and lunar, stating that the Moon and all other Planets shine when they reflect sunlight. Rather than accepting the explanation that Rahu and Ketu created the eclipses, he stated that the shadows were actually caused by shadows that were cast by Earth. The lunar eclipse, he stated, would occur when the Moon entered the earth's shadow.

He also calculated out the sidereal rotation, the rotation of the Earth when in reference to the fixed stars, like 23 hours, 56 minutes, and 4.1 seconds. This put his calculation at the exact value of a sidereal year as 365 days, 6 hours, 12 minutes, and 30 seconds. His error was only that of 3 minutes and 20 seconds from what we know is the value today.

# Chapter 6: Creating Your Vedic Astrology Chart

Now, at this point, we have explained plenty about the background of the Vedas. We have gone over influential figures. We have discussed the key factors. Now, it is time to start looking at creating your own Vedic astrology chart. Now, keep in mind that this is highly difficult by hand, especially due to the fact that you will have to go over the various Planets and figure out exactly where they were when you were born. Additionally, you must do so from where you are born as well.

Nowadays, mapping out your Vedic astrology natal chart by hand is outdated. You would need a few hours of time, some significant math skills, and an ephemeris or the year that you were born, as well as for the years of anyone else that you wish to calculate it out for. This can be very difficult to do, and there is very little margin of error. If you do not calculate this out correctly, you can run into additional issues that make your chart inaccurate. Those such inaccuracies can be hugely problematic for you, and because of that, they will not actually give you the proper readings. You could end up with a reading that actually places your Planets in the wrong houses. You could have issues with trying to figure out where to put things, or you might even just struggle with the math.

Because modern science and technology are so incredibly beneficial, there are now several calculators that you can use that will help you to get the details. Most of these also will not require you to put in any identifying information either. You simply input your birthdate, your time of birth, your location of birth, and sometimes, your name or first initial. The calculators then run all of the calculations for you, and the end result is that you get a reading for the time of your birth.

They will usually, at the very least, provide you with the placements of all of your signs and Planets in the appropriate Houses so you can be certain that you have an accurate representation. However, most of the free sites won't actually tell you how you can decipher what these planetary signs actually mean for you.

In the previous book, we discussed reading the Houses, the Planets in Houses, and the general ways to read these as well. This should have provided you with a basic, generic reading of what you can expect, especially within the Houses. This is good for just getting started, as well as having a solid understanding of what the various signs and symbols mean within the various Planets and houses.

In this chapter, however, we are going to address several of the ways that you can expect to look at the information. We will first go over what you should expect if you have gotten your hands on the appropriate information to start filling in your own natal chart by hand, and then we will start discussing what you should do to fill it out and begin reading the charts as well.

This is a fantastic first step into beginning your understanding of Vedic astrology and the charts that are created for you. If you are ready to get started, then you are certainly in the right place. Keep in mind that this chapter is all about filling in the information. If you want to start interpreting the information, you will need to consult the guide in Chapter 8 in this book, as well as the guides to reading the Planets in the previous book, if you need a refresher. Remember, the information in this book is meant to go into further depth. It is meant to provide you with more of an understanding of your chart rather than revisiting the same material. If you need to check back, then feel free to do so.

## Creating Your Chart by Hand

## Creating Your Vedic Astrology Chart

To create your chart by hand, it is strongly recommended that you use the Internet to pick up an ephemeris for the year that you were born. However, remember that this is not going to be as accurate as simply entering into a calculator on your computer just due to the fact that location matters immensely with your ascendant, and sometimes, even with placements.

To do this, you would need the ephemeris first, and you would then go along and look at the date of your birth. What are the placements of the various planets? You would select each placement of each Planet on the Ephemeris and then place it where it belongs on the chart in the appropriate House.

You know which House is which on your chart quite simply—it is divided based upon degrees of the circle. Remember, there are 360 degrees in the Zodiac. Each sign, and each house, gets 30 degrees of that circle to create the whole thing. The Houses are as followed:

| House | Degrees |
| --- | --- |
| 1st House | 0-29 degrees |
| 2nd House | 30-59 degrees |
| 3rd House | 60-89 degrees |
| 4th House | 90-119 degrees |
| 5th House | 120-149 degrees |
| 6th House | 150-179 degrees |
| 7th House | 180-209 degrees |
| 8th House | 210-239 degrees |
| 9th House | 240-269 degrees |
| 10th House | 270-299 degrees |
| 11th House | 300-329 degrees |
| 12th House | 330-359 degrees |

As you track where things fall on the ephemeris, you can then begin placing them in the appropriate charts on your birth chart as well. The birth chart that you create should have all of the space for you right built into it.

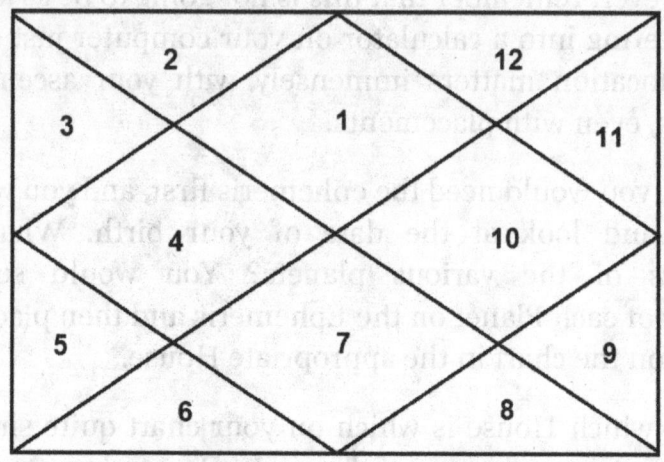

Following the above guide, you would track the Planets to the right locations and then place them into your chart. For example, if the Sun is at 56 degrees at that point of birth, then it would be in your 2nd House. Continue this process until all of your Planets have been placed.

Once you have the Planets placed, you must do the same for the Constellations. This is where things get tricky—to do this, you will first need to get your Ascendant. Once you have your Ascendant, everything else falls in order just due to the fact that the Zodiac moves in a linear line across the sky and across space. Keep in mind that the Ascendant is going to be regularly changing, so accuracy matters. Where the constellations appear to be and which one is on the horizon depends on the Earth's orbit, so you will need this done exactly. Again, you can use online calculators that will customize this for a truly reliable result that you can use. You will be able to

Let's say that your Ascendant sign is Taurus. That goes into your 1st House. From there, you follow along the line. The order of the Zodiac then begins from there. If Taurus is in your 1st house, then the 2nd house has Gemini, the 3rd has Cancer, and so on, all the way to your 12th house of Aries.

When you have all of your signs, your Planets, and your houses sorted out, you can start comparing information. Again, it is far easier to simply turn to a digital chart and use that to fill in everything for you. This way, you do not have to worry about the accuracy—a computer does all of the calculations for you, and you will get great results without any of the guesswork.

## The Houses

The first thing that you will do is read your houses. Once you have your chart all lined up, it becomes important to take a look at what happens when certain signs and certain Planets are in certain Houses. Some Houses will exalt the Planets and Signs. Others will cause all sorts of issues, and finding out what happens based upon the various combinations will matter immensely. When you go through the various matchups, you may start to see some inherent compatibilities or incompatibilities as well. You want to make sure that you know how your Houses are interacting with the Signs and the Planets. This is the most basic understanding that you can use. It will start to give you a general overview of your primary houses and parts of life. Remember, each House is going to correspond with a different aspect of your life as well. You will need to pay attention to each House and consider them all in the context of the individual. As a reminder, each house represents:

| House | Meaning |
|---|---|
| 1st House | The self, the body, life in general |
| 2nd House | Wealth and speech |

| | |
|---|---|
| 3rd House | Courage and siblings |
| 4th House | Home, family, and mothers |
| 5th House | Intelligence, children |
| 6th House | Enemies, worries |
| 7th House | Spouse, desires |
| 8th House | Longevity, vulnerability |
| 9th House | Higher learning, dharma |
| 10th House | Profession, reputation |
| 11th House | Gains |
| 12th House | Enlightenment and death |

You will take a look at each house in depth. As you do so, comparing the results of your signs and your Planets, you may want to consider writing up notes as you go along. Take note of the important interactions to help you keep track. As you are learning, it can be very difficult to track everything, so the notes are helpful.

When you have gotten a good idea of your various House readings and what happens to each of yours with the current layout that you have, it is time to start moving on. Pay attention to what happens with each House in relation to each of your Signs.

Next comes the Aspects. You will need to consider the influence of the Planets in their current positions and how they interact with those around them. Again, this was a concept provided to you in the previous book. As you continue to put together your Natal chart, you start to see all sorts of information. The Aspects allow you to see all sorts of information that you might not usually consider as well. For example, consider the 7th House for a moment—this is the House of Marriage. When Saturn is residing in this house, they are likely to delay the marriage.

You must then start considering conjunctions as well. Conjunctions occur when you have two Planets in the same House to the same degree. When you have this in the same nakshatra, then you get conjunction. These start to interact with each other as well, and you must also consider what happens.

You will also need to take a look at any retrograde Planets as well. These are Planets that are traveling backward rather than forwards in their orbits. While they are not truly moving backward, thanks to the movements of the Earth and the movements of the Planets themselves, it appears as if they are moving backward at the time. Remember, these retrograde Planets can create strange effects on the Planet in mind as well.

## Reading the Signs in the Planets

Next, it is time to start considering the interactions between the Signs and the Planets. What happens to each of your Signs when they are on certain Planets? There are all sorts of things that interact with these. You must consider the Lord of each Sign so you can see how they do when they are with the Planet. Imagine that you have Taurus and Jupiter together. Taurus is ruled by Venus. Venus and Jupiter share a neutral relationship together, and thus, the sign and planet, when combined, create a very neutral reaction. Together, they are going to interact in certain ways.

Generally speaking, two friendly Planets will make friendly outcomes for the native—they will provide you with plenty of good benefits based upon the individual. The various signs will create all sorts of interactions with the various Planets, all dependent upon how the Planets and the Signs are able to relate to each other. Some signs will exalt or debilitate a Planet, regardless of the relationship with the Lord of the sign and the Planet in mind.

Considering this relationship will help you immensely with understanding more. It should allow you to start recognizing what happens next and what you can expect along the way as well. You will be able to start gaining all sorts of information as you look for the way that the signs and Planets start to interact with each other.

You will get a comprehensive guide to all of the different reactions of signs and Planets when put together, and you will want to take a good look at this when you are going over your chart. This will provide plenty of crucial information that can help you, especially if you start discovering what happens with each.

## Reading the Yogas

As you continue down your chart, you will also want to study the Yogas in your chart as well. These will give you specific combinations of Planets that come together and make very specific effects. The effects only happen when the criteria are spelled out exactly. For example, consider the Bhadra Yoga. This occurs only when Mercury is in Kendra and put into Aries or exaltation. When this happens, the Bhadra Yoga occurs. This then creates the typical Bhadra Yoga signs, such as eloquence and intelligence.

As with understanding the Signs, there is plenty of information in the next chapter about reading the main Yogas as well. You will want to check these out to determine if any of them fall onto your chart. If they are on your chart, take a look at what they mean. They can be good or bad depending upon the combination, and you will want to know what to expect later on. However, if you don't stop and consider this, you might be missing out on some very important information. We will go over the yogas shortly so you can catch on to whatever the ones playing on your chart will be and what you can expect from them.

# Chapter 7: Using Your Vedic Astrology Chart

Life is difficult enough without any additional complications added to it. We have to understand what we are doing. We have to choose a job, choose a partner, try to live life, and figure out what is just right for us. However, if everything is all related and it all comes back to Karma and teaching us the lessons that we need to learn in order to achieve enlightenment, how is it that we are supposed to find ways that we can live the right life for us? How are we supposed to know if we are making good choices or if the choices that we have chosen are actually highly problematic for us? It is difficult—but it doesn't have to be.

You can learn to understand what it is that the Universe has in store for you. You can learn to start seeing what it is that you can do to help yourself and better yourself. You can work on figuring out how to work with yourself and the fate that you have. You can start looking at the way that the Universe is going to work with you. And no, you don't have to be a mind reader or psychic to do so—you can simply look at your Vedic astrology natal chart. Looking at the natal chart, you will start seeing this information spelled out for you.

Each person is unique. Each situation that people are in is unique. At the moment of your birth, the skies aligned in a way that is supposed to be telling of your history. It will tell you of your fate and what you can start to expect. Being able to see that you have the power to understand yourself means that you should be able to start looking better into the future. You can start to recognize the messages that the universe wants to send you, and then you can use that information to make sure that you make the best choices for yourself. You can start making the decisions that will help you to do better.

In this chapter, we are going to start considering several of the uses that you can consider for your own chart. We will be going over what you can expect to use these charts to influence your own lives. These charts are held in very high regard and should be treated as such.

## Life Prediction

Generally speaking, people stop and look at their charts because that allows them to start seeing the future. When you look at someone's birth chart, you can start seeing what to expect. Imagine that someone is born with a placement that implies that they are likely to thrive—they generally can know to expect primarily good things from themselves and their charts. They are able to make sure that they are on track, and they are able to keep themselves generally happy. They can have a pretty solid idea that life will not be significantly rough for them because their placements are generally positive.

On the other hand, if someone has a very unfortunate combination, they have answers when they are constantly struggling. They have answers that will help them to understand exactly why they are having so many issues the way that they have been. They can start to understand which Planets are having these negative effects, and because they can see the reasoning behind it, they can then start to apply those changes as well. They can start looking at the ways that they are able to do better. They can start seeing how they are able to balance out issues with their actions. They can appease the poorly placed Planets and start trying to fix the issues.

Being able to have a general prediction of how life goes means that nothing is ever much of a surprise. The reason that some believe that checking their charts so often matters so much is that just about every large event and milestone in their lives requires a consultation by being able to turn to that chart and understand what to expect means that life is that much easier to navigate. If you know that you tend to be very adventurous and you are applying for jobs, for example, you would probably want to avoid jobs that are very monotonous because you know that your chart does not look kindly on the idea of sitting around when there are things that you could be doing instead.

Keep in mind that these charts are quite detailed and filled with all sorts of crucial information that can help you immensely. These charts will tell you about every aspect of your life that is meaningful or important. They will help you to see the ins and outs that are underneath the initial occurrences around you. You may not know what to expect at first, but looking at your chart can give you that idea in just about every aspect of your life.

This is why you have twelve houses. Each house is ruled by something different, and that will allow you to start understanding what will happen throughout your life. From how healthy you are likely to be to how much you will struggle, it is all in the Planets, and all you have to do is look to them to succeed.

## Marriage

Marriage is one of those more important aspects of life that people tend to look to the skies for. Your marriage is so important in your life that it becomes something that must be double-checked for compatibility. It is believed that your chart will actually influence how long you will get along with certain people. If two people have conflicting charts, they are likely to struggle. Two people with combinations that are auspicious, however, are likely to enjoy life together and enjoy their marriages. For this reason and because marriage is one of the most important aspects of life, being able to check out how likely you are to get along with someone else matters. In fact, in arranged marriages, they are done primarily by compatibility in the charts.

Your marriage is one of the most important relationships in your life. If it is not well-matched and if you have a partner that is not actually going to be beneficial to you or compatible with you, then you have serious issues. You run the risk of even getting divorced, which could cause problems. Divorces, even if amicable, are hugely problematic. It could be an issue if you were to, for example, have children, and those children end up going from home to home. It could also be problematic if you were to have to detangle finances, move, and the like.

Being certain that your emotional connection to your spouse is solid and going to be beneficial matters immensely. There is so much hinging upon you having a successful, comfortable marriage that you want to do right the first time. You want to double-check that your spouse will be one that is not only compatible with you, but you will be compatible with them as well.

## To Understand Karma

It is said that at the moment of your birth, your karma is written, and it is all spelled out in the sky. It is something that will help you immensely. Karma allows you to see the understanding of your past lives as well as what you can expect in your current one. It helps you to start seeing what you are going to have to do and where you are going to have to go in your life to be successful and to be confident.

Karma is the fundamental factor in Hinduism that drives everything. The ultimate goal in life is to achieve that success and salvation, and it is not possible to get that salvation and enlightenment until you have learned everything that the Universe has to teach you. It is not until you know what you are doing and how you are doing it that you start to finally get that progress.

Karma has a strange way of sneaking up on us when we least expect it. However, it is all right there, if you know where to look. If you know what to expect and where to look, you know that you can turn to the stars and view your karma's past and future. Look to the areas in your life that may be unfavorable. Saturn in 7, for example, causes problems with marriage. It could delay it. There are house and combinations that may imply that your health may not be the best, and others that show your relationships with other family members as well. When you start seeing this and taking a look at the ways that you can read your karma in your chart, you start seeing where you may need to make some changes. After all, karma will continue to repeat itself until you figure out what the message that it is trying to teach you are. It is only then, when the message is accepted, and you start to make the changes in your life, that you start to see that you are able to move past those struggles.

## To Understand Health

If you have always wanted to know what your health is going to look like, you are in luck. Being able to glance at the stars might sound too good to be true, but certain combinations are known to be related directly to the individual's health. It can be seen that certain Planets are directly linked to poorer health when they are in certain aspects and houses. Likewise, other houses may represent good fortune and health as well. It becomes essential that you understand and know what the most common signs to pay attention to are. It is imperative that you stop and see what it is that you can do to start lessening the potentially bad effects. Let's say you've got a sign that shows that you are likely to suffer and be sick a lot. By knowing this, you can then make it a point to try your hardest to remain as healthy as possible to prevent an untimely demise. This helps you to ensure that you are in your best possible condition, in hopes that you will be able to prevent yourself from getting sick later on.

If you know that you are likely to get sick as well, you may be able to watch closely for signs that you are getting sick. In paying attention to the fact that you are prone to illness, you should be able to find yourself working to keep yourself healthier just because you can get treated earlier. If you are prone to ear infections and your ear is sore, you would probably simply call in a prescription and pick it up, no fuss attached, to heal yourself. Instead of waiting to see if it would subside, you would get it treated sooner because you knew what to expect.

Being able to see how likely you are to remain healthy means that you can take care of yourself and vice versa. It can let you know when treating yourself and taking better care of yourself can really become important as well. This is the perfect way for you to ensure that you are on the right track to keep yourself happy and healthy, or at the very least, take care of yourself, so you know that you will survive.

## To Understand Finances

Our finances in life can be difficult, to say the least. They are dependent upon work, jobs, locale, and more. We all want to live with the money that we would need to pay for our day to day expenses. However, some want more than that, as well. Some are driven by their insatiable need for wealth and fame, and the individuals who do need wealth might want to know what they can do to earn it, too. Thankfully, there is a simple answer to this—understanding finances by looking at your chart.

When you look at your birth chart, you get all sorts of information about your financial situation. You will discover if you are likely to have some sort of career affinity that will afford you that wealth. For example, you may be perfect to be a teacher, or you might be the right kind of person to teach or be a leader or politician. By being able to see the various effects, you can start figuring out what is going to work best for you, and you can start pursuing careers that are going to be meaningful, or at the very least, compatible with you and the way that the stars have aligned.

By choosing out work that is based upon your charts, you can start picking out those careers that you are likely to excel in. You may be surprised by the options that are written out there for you, but give them a shot. Let yourself give it a try at least once to see if it does happen to resonate with you. You might be surprised that the right career for you that will bring you that financial success that you are looking for involves you doing something that you never in a million years would have considered. However, remember, sometimes, the stars are there to surprise you. Sometimes, they work in mysterious ways that you cannot quite understand until they have fully unfolded themselves to create the intended effect. At the very least, you owe it to yourself at least once to try the career or field that has been suggested by your chart. You may be surprised to find that the career for you is something different. You may also find that the career that you love, but are struggling financially in, is not the right one for you either.

## To Understand Family Life

Your family life is deeply ingrained into your entire chart. From each of your Houses relating to one of your relationships with a family member to there being so much emphasis on relationships with each of the signs that you have, this particular purpose is highly important as well. If you have a conflict with your parents, this could be the reason for it. Understanding what that means and what you can expect to experience means that you can start understanding those familial relationships better as well. You will be able to ensure that your relationships with everyone around you are actually beneficial to you. When you do this enough, you start to see that there are very clear aspects that you will need to consider. You will need to pay attention to the fact that some relationships simply will be doomed to fail or struggle.

When you look at the relationships that you have, you should start seeing the patterns, and you may realize the patterns that you have in your relationships. Viewing the various placements of your houses will help you to see what it is that you can expect with your parents, your siblings, and more.

You might be able to change some of what you do. You should be able to start changing the relationships that you have so you will be able to connect better. Or, you can simply accept the way that the stars have influenced you.

## To Understand General Skills

As you may notice as you read over the various placements of constellations, there are very clear skills that are outlined. Certain people have certain skills, and they tend to be influenced by the stars that the individual has. When you go over the various stars and planets, you may start to see certain skills manifest. When you go over the skills that you have, you should be able to understand where best to emphasize your skills and practices. The more that you work on yourself, you should start understanding yourself. You should be able to see that your skills will work well for you.

Considering what your natural skills are will also help you in other aspects of your life as well. The more that you look into your skills and the more that you were to emphasize and build those skills, the more likely you are to better yourself. You might be able to see that the skills that you are neglecting the most are actually the skills that you should be bettering. Appeal to the general skills that your chart says that you are likely to do well. Make sure that you work on them and see what happens. You may be pleasantly surprised.

# Chapter 8: Reading Your Chart in the Sky

When you are ready to get started in Vedic astrology, one of the first places that you will look is at your birth chart. The birth chart that you create is going to strongly influence the person that you are. It will create all sorts of great changes to the way that you behave, how your family treats you, how your family does in general, and even will play a part in your general successes.

In the previous book, you learned to recognize the basics. You learned to see and understand what a birth chart was, and then to recognize several important factors. You learned to recognize the ascendant, significators, and discussed exaltation and debilitation. From there, you learned about the Planets themselves and information about what they represent. These representations, when taken in the context of houses, helps you to start to understand more about how to read your own individual birth chart. However, we only scratched the surface of what your chart has to offer you. Yes, you have to look at where the Planets fall and which houses they are in, as well as which signs are also in those houses. However, you also have to look at how the different positions tend to play off of each other as well.

You want to make sure that you are looking at everything from how the various Planets position themselves in relation to other planets. Certain combinations can create certain effects that may be unexpected but are incredibly important to know and recognize. They are known as the yogas.

You will also need to take a look at the Nakshatras again as well. Remember, these are your lunar constellations, and they create all sorts of alterations that you will need to consider. From showing the way that the Moon changes and the signs that it travels through, you will begin to see more information that you need. Each lunar constellation passes through four phases, or padas, as they travel across the sky, and being able to see those tracks and recognize how they travel matters immensely in how they present in the people born under them.

Finally, you must also be willing to look at what it means when each plate passes through each constellation as well. This allows you to get more nuance out of your birth chart readings as well as to get more accuracy that you can use.

Ultimately, being able to read birth charts matters immensely. If you are new to Vedic astrology and none of what was mentioned in this section so far has made any sense, then you should probably revisit the intro level book to start getting that basic information. The basics matter, but remember, this chapter is written assuming you already know how to read a chart and that you already understand terminology like "exalted" or "combusted in regards to a planet's placement on the chart that it is on. You will need to have this understanding so you can be certain that you can read what you will see here and put it into action.

## Revisiting the Nakshatras

Remember, the Nakshatras are the lunar constellations. They are the ways that the Moon changes throughout the month, and they influence the people within them. The Nakshatras take 28 days to move through all twelve zodiac signs. This helps you to understand the intuition and intelligence, and it influences the emotions that you have as well.

As we go through all of the Nakshatras, we will be taking a look at some important information. In particular, we will take a look at the characteristics of each type of person born under these different nakshatras, as well as what happens in each of the padas for each of the Nakshatras.

The padas are each just one-fourth of each phase. However, each pada is ruled by a navamsa. The navamsa is the equivalent of 1/16 of a sign, allowing you to see more precisely where on a chart that particular sign is. Some are considered quite fortunate, while others can be harmful as well. We will be taking a look now at the Nakshatras and their padas and those positions.

## Ashwini

*Astronomical name: Beta Arietis*
*Deity: Ashwini Kumaras*
*Lord: Ketu*
*Symbol: Horseman*
*Color: Blood red*
*Gemstone: Cat's eye red*
*Shakti: Reaching things quickly*
*Caste: Vyshya*
*Nature: Light*
*Rashi: Aries sign*

*Male characteristics*

Men born in the Ashwini Nakshatra tend to be handsome. They'll have broad foreheads, big noses, and bright eyes. He will be a great friend, patient, and grateful. However, when his patience does snap, he can be difficult to rein in. He is sometimes afraid of criticism to the point that he would be considered paranoid.

He loves his family greatly, but sometimes, his humiliation gets in the way. He tends to struggle in gaining love from his father and is much more likely to connect to maternal uncles. His friends will help him more than his family, and he is likely to marry between the ages of 26 and 30. Typically, he has more sons than daughters.

*Female characteristics*

Women born under the Ashwini Nakshatra tend to win people over with their words. They are patient, pure-hearted, and loving, but they also tend to have a higher libido, and that can interfere with them. They tend to respect tradition and their elders. Typically, they will work in administrative work and devote themselves, but they will also quit focusing more on the family.

She will probably marry between 23 and 26 years of age, and if outside of that range, they are likely to have issues. Typically, relationships for those with Ashwini nakshatra tend to struggle in general, and the love life is cursed to suffer from divorce or possibly even death.

*First Pada*

Ashwini nakshatra in 1$^{st}$ pada falls into Aries navamsa, governed by Mars. This is noted as being representative of courage, vigorous activity, and independence. It is blessed with initiative and energy.

*Second Pada*

Ashwini nakshatra in 2$^{nd}$ pada falls in Taurus Navamsa, governed by Venus. It is noted as being ruled by practicality and resourcefulness thanks to its association with everything graceful about the Ashvini Kumaras. The manifestations of thoughts and ideas will come through in this pada.

*Third Pada*

Ashwini Nakshatra in 3rd pada falls into Gemini Navamsa, governed by Mercury. It is representative of communication and humor. In this pada, you will see quick decision-making and outstanding skill in mental activities.

*Fourth Pada*

Ashwini Nakshatra in 4th pada falls into the Cancer Navamsa. It is ruled by the moon. In particular, you will see an emphasis on both physical and mental healing in this pada, and it will manifest compassion in the native.

# Bharani

*Astronomical name: 35 Arietis*
*Deity: Yama*
*Lord: Venus*
*Color: Blood red*
*Gemstone: Diamond*

*Male characteristics*

Males born under Bharani tend not to be as likable. Though they care about people and are true to their need to keep people safe, they tend to lose favor. They are outspoken and will say the truth, regardless of how it hurts. They are driven by following their conscience and will do what they think is right, no matter what. They are also quite forgiving when someone approaches them genuinely with an apology.

Typically, they will see that they have better circumstances after the age of 33, but for the most part, they are well-rounded and suited well to just about any position. They love their family and are adamant in their love. Typically, they will marry between 26 and 30 years.

*Female characteristics*

Female Bharani natives are considered pure and modest. They are respectful but independent-minded. They will do what works best for them. She may be bold and sometimes even err on the side of impulsive. She is likely to be independent and work for herself or as a receptionist. She is likely to get married around the age of 23 and is likely to be dominant in the home, with the trust of her spouse.

*First Pada*

The first pada is in the Leo Navamsa and is ruled primarily by the sun. This, in particular, emphasizes creativity, to the point that it becomes all-encompassing for the native. They can be selfish and hurt others without knowing it.

*Second Pada*

The second pada is in the Virgo Navamsa and is ruled by Mercury. The focus, in particular here, is on working hard, and this person is likely to be quite altruistic. They are typically in control of themselves at all times, even when they are surrounded by chaos.

*Third Pada*

The third pada is in the Libra Navamsa, and it is ruled by Venus. This particular combination creates natives that have the skill to balance out opposites. However, they can also find themselves distracted by their libidos, regardless of how bad it may be for them.

*Fourth Pada*

Finally, the fourth pada is in the Scorpio Navamsa. It is governed by Mars. This native is someone who is going to be filled with energy and productivity. They have issues influencing that energy sometimes, however, and they have to work hard to figure out how best to funnel that energy so it is used effectively.

# Krittika

*Astronomical name: Eta Tauri*
*Deity: Agni*
*Lord: Sun*
*Color: White*
*Gemstone: Ruby*

*Male characteristics*

The male born under Krittika Nakshatra is generally quite intelligent. However, his impatience tends to make it harder for him to ever actually finish anything. He does manage to stop and give other people good advice, and he tends to be a great friend. However, he is likely to discard friendships that stand in his way.

*Female characteristics*

Krittika women tend to be highly intelligent. They focus on how they could withstand any sort of emotional blackmail, and they are emotionally resilient. However, that is sometimes misunderstood as arrogance, causing problems for her. May end up being housewives, but they struggle to be happy in their positions that they have.

*First Pada*

In the first pada, the Nakshatra is in the Sagittarius Navamsa. It is governed by Jupiter. It creates an influence on generosity and courage. These people may be interested in military careers.

*Second Pada*

In the second pada, the Krittika Nakshatra is in Capricorn Navamsa. It is ruled by Saturn. Here, the focus is on material ethics over spirituality.

*Third Pada*

The third pada is in the Aquarius Navamsa and is ruled by Saturn. It is considered to be indicative of generosity and compassion, and the individual is likely to focus on accumulating knowledge.

*Fourth Pada*

The fourth pada is in the Pisces Navamsa and is governed by Jupiter. Here, you can expect to see the individual behave in ways that are conscious of material comforts. They will pursue ways that they can be physically comfortable above all else.

# Rohini

*Astronomical name: Aldebaran*
*Deity: Brahma*
*Lord: Moon*
*Color: White*
*Gemstone: Natural Pearl*

*Male characteristics*

Males born under Rohini tend to be hot-tempered, and that makes him difficult to control. He is likely to struggle with balancing other people's opinions and mostly cares more about himself and his own personal frame of mind. He is most likely to criticize others and is driven to follow his heart rather than his mind. However, this helps him to love hard and makes him willing to sacrifice for just about anyone.

*Female characteristics*

Female natives of Rohini Nakshatra tend to be both well-mannered and well-dressed. They might be weak emotionally, but she is great at putting on that façade that will help her to make others believe the opposite. However, she can be almost violent when provoked. She will love her family and children and find that she is fulfilled by her family life.

*First Pada*

The first pada of Rohini Nakshatra is within the Aries Navamsa and is governed by Mars. In particular, these natives will focus on needing to gain physical pleasures. However, their reverence for money also tends to lead them to be generous as well.

*Second Pada*

In the second pada, the Rohini Nakshatra is in the Taurus Navamsa. It is ruled by Venus. Natives under this Nakshatra tend to be courageous but also somewhat materialistic at the same time. They can fend off adversities, but they usually do so on their own terms.

*Third Pada*

The third pada is found in the Gemini Navamsa and is ruled by Mercury. It creates an influence of power in arts and in business, and typically, these natives are quite wealthy.

*Fourth Pada*

The fourth pada is found in the Cancer Navamsa and is ruled by the Moon. Here, there is an emphasis on both material and domestic comforts. In this phase, travel can be quite lucrative.

# Mrigashira

*Astronomical name: Lambda Orionis*
*Deity: Chandra*
*Lord: Mars*
*Color: Silver-grey*
*Gemstone: Red coral*

*Male characteristics*

Males born under this sign tend to be doubting in nature. However, they will always turn to their own honesty. They will do what they can to be honest with other people. He may not follow the advice that he gives others, but he tends to give great advice to others.

*Female characteristics*

Women born under this sign tend to emphasize charity work. She may be alert and witty, but she may also show signs of selfishness. She may speak before she thinks, much to the detriment of others. She can cause serious harm in how she behaves. Nevertheless, she finds herself to be a doting and devoted mother and wife.

*First Pada*

This pada is ruled by Leo Navamsa and the Sun. When born under this sign, the native is likely to express themselves creatively most of the time.

*Second Pada*

This pada is in the Virgo Navamsa and is governed by Mercury. Those born here tend to focus on being humorous but also showing a degree of cunning calculations. Typically, these natives are quite smart.

*Third Pada*

The third pada is in the Libra Navamsa and is ruled by Venus. This native is likely to feel driven to find relationships that are emotionally and mentally stimulating.

*Fourth Pada*

The fourth pada is found in the Scorpio Navamsa and is governed by Mars. This native is likely to be very intellectual and superficial in many aspects.

# Ardra

*Astronomical name: Alpha Orionis*
*Deity: Rudra*
*Lord: Rahu*
*Color: Green*
*Gemstone: Gomedh*

*Male characteristics*

Males under the Ardra Nakshatra are typically very well-rounded. They have the knowledge that they would need to be skilled in a lot of aspects. They are typically compassionate and calm, and even when things get rough, they tend to maintain their level-headedness. They are typically going to multitask often and may cause problems because they cannot focus well. They settle down and work away from their home most of the time.

## Female characteristics

Females in this Nakshatra tend to be very peaceful. They typically are cheap, intelligent, and sometimes fussy about what they are doing. She is likely to be quite smart as well and may be an engineer or a pharmacist. She tends to devote herself to work and may get married late. She is not likely to find happiness in her family.

## First Pada

The first pada is found in the Sagittarius Navamsa. It is ruled by Jupiter. In this phase, the native is likely to be curious and love to explore. They may be relaxed but also prone to collecting material goods.

## Second Pada

The second pada is in Capricorn and is ruled by Saturn. This particular Nakshatra is representative of material ambitions and sometimes even frustration. Typically, the negative qualities in this Nakshatra will manifest most in this quarter. It is generally inauspicious.

## Third Pada

The third pada is in Aquarius and is governed by Saturn. It tends to represent a scientific nature. However, it can still be quite inauspicious as well, and there are sometimes intense thoughts.

## Fourth Pada

The fourth pada is in the Pisces Navamsa. It is ruled by Jupiter. This particular pada tends to represent sensitivity and compassion. There will be an urge to be compassionate toward others that may be less privileged, and that is important.

## Punarvasu

*Astronomical name: Beta Geminorium*
*Deity: Adity*
*Lord: Jupiter*
*Color: Lead*
*Gemstone: Yellow sapphire*

*Male characteristics*

This native is typically quite religious. He is typically very well behaved in his childhood, but as he ages, he tends to become more arrogant and hot-headed. He may be a little hard to understand sometimes, but he may also crave things that are difficult to reach.

*Female characteristics*

Females born under this Nakshatra are typically calm, but sometimes even cutting at times. She may cause problems with her neighbors and relatives thanks to how she acts at times, but she also knows that she has to give respect where respect is due.

*First Pada*

The first pada is in Aries Navamsa and is ruled by Mars. It emphasizes a focus on adventure and camaraderie.

*Second Pada*

The second pada is found in the Taurus Navamsa. It is ruled by Venus. Those native to this position tend to be earthy and focus on material comforts whenever possible.

*Third Pada*

The third pada is typically recognized as being in the Gemini Navamsa and is governed by Mercury. This particular pada puts a focus on mental actions and activities such as imagination.

*Fourth Pada*

The fourth pada is in the Cancer Navamsa and is governed by the Moon. This focus is on the strength and nurturing spirit as well as helping the needy.

## Pushya

*Astronomical name: Delta Cancri*
*Deity: Brihaspathi*
*Lord: Saturn*
*Color: Black mixed with red*
*Gemstone: Blue Sapphire*

*Male characteristics*

Men born under this Nakshatra tend to be very emotionally weak at times. It is difficult for him to figure out what to choose, and though he may have good behaviors, those behaviors tend to have secondary motives that will help him to get his way. He is typically hypocritical because he is quite negative inside but tends to pretend to be positive to help to build his ego.

*Female characteristics*

Females under this Nakshatra typically find themselves constantly in turmoil. She may be very charming and peaceful, as well as submissive, but she is treated poorly in return. Getting peace is difficult to achieve, and it can be difficult for her. She is likely to struggle in the family that she is married into, despite her devotion and attempts to work with their traditions.

*First Pada*

The first pada is in the Leo Navamsa and is governed by the sun. This particular alignment creates someone who is focused on achievement, riches, family, and pride in one's ancestors. It is strongly supported by the Planets.

*Second Pada*

The second pada is found in the Virgo Navamsa and is ruled by Mercury. It creates a focus on the achievements of hard-working professionals and creates people who are likely to see good results.

*Third Pada*

The third pada is found in the Libra Navamsa and is ruled by Venus. This particular pada creates someone who is going to focus on the home, luxury, and other physical comforts. Typically, there is a favor from Mercury, Venus, Saturn, and the Moon.

*Fourth Pada*

The fourth pada is found in the Scorpio Navamsa and is ruled by Mars. It tends to show a connection with celestial powers. However, it may also manifest in negative traits as well, such as causing dependence or intolerance.

# Ashlesha

*Astronomical name: Alpha Hydrae*
*Deity: Nagas*
*Lord: Mercury*
*Color: Black mixed with red*
*Gemstone: Emerald*

*Male characteristics*

This Nakshatra creates men who are not grateful. Rather, they tend to err on the side of deception in that they may act as if they are compassionate, but it is more for show than anything else. He is great at navigating through the social nuances, but he has very little concern for people. He does not discriminate, however, and that means that he is generally fit for those rules of ruling fairly.

*Female characteristics*

Females born under this Nakshatra tend to be self-controlled but are also less likely to be caring about others. They are quite shy but also willing to win an argument by mastering the words that they use.

*First Pada*

The first pada is in the Sagittarius Navamsa and is controlled by Jupiter. It is typically going to create people who work hard and show dedication. Typically, they may show signs of enemies and struggle with their health.

*Second Pada*

The second pada is in the Capricorn Navamsa and is ruled by Saturn. This quarter is found and marked by ambitions clinging to one's possessions.

*Third Pada*

The third pada is in the Aquarius Navamsa and is also ruled by Saturn. This particular Navamsa is typically linked to secrecy and occult.

*Fourth Pada*

The fourth pada is in the Pisces Navamsa and is also ruled by Jupiter. This particular pada is typically recognized as a war between morals. This is the pada in which you will see the Ashlesha serpent slain. During this pada, people may struggle with influence over others.

# Magha

*Astronomical name: Regulus*
*Deity: Pithras*
*Lord: Ketu*
*Color: Ivory or cream*
*Gemstone: Cat's Eye*

*Male characteristics*

Men born under this sign tend to be very industrious. They typically hold their elders in high regard and are usually soft-spoken and happy-go-lucky. They allow themselves to work mostly with other people, and they love making sure that their relationships with others are genuine and beneficial for all involved.

*Female characteristics*

Females born under this sign tend to be very combative. They tend to be fond of arguing and may also present with shorter tempers, but they are also typically quite generous. They typically love material comforts and focus on both their domestic and professional lives. She is likely to be very spiritually inclined and tends to help others.

*First Pada*

The first pada of the Magha Nakshatra is in the Aries Navamsa, ruled by Mars. There is a focus on will-power here.

*Second Pada*

The second pada is in the Taurus sign and is ruled by Venus. This particular pada emphasizes duty, and those born under it tend to be good and present good images to those around them.

*Third Pada*

The third pada is found in the Gemini Navamsa and is ruled by Mercury. This particular one puts an emphasis on the pursuit of artistic endeavors, as well as scholarly pursuits. Typically, there is an emphasis on knowledge, learning, and other similar mental activities.

*Fourth Pada*

The fourth pada is in the Cancer Navamsa, and it is ruled by the moon. This placement emphasizes the need for family pride and ancestor worship. These natives love rituals and ritualistic practices.

## Purva Phalguni

*Astronomical name: Delta Leonis*
*Deity: Bhaga*
*Lord: Venus*
*Color: Light brown*
*Gemstone: Diamond*

*Male characteristics*

Men born under this sign tend to love their freedom and resent the attempts made to slow it down. These natives usually find that they can command and maintain fame in their desired fields, and that is something that they can use to their advantage. They are prone to feeling disturbed by it, however, and possess the intuitive power that they will need to help them. They are usually able to use their intuition in a positive manner.

*Female characteristics*

Females born under this sign tend to be very polite, chaste, and intelligent, especially in regards to the arts. They are likely to donate their time and money to charities or charitable actions, and they make it a point to only act in ways that they deem to be righteous. However, she may also be a bit of a showoff and need that recognition to feel better about herself.

*First Pada*

The first pada is in the Leo Navamsa. It is governed by the Sun. This particular pada represents the self. Those who are intelligent can use that intelligence to help to educate those around them.

*Second Pada*

The second pada is in the Virgo Navamsa and is governed by Mercury. This particular phase is going to emphasize the hardworking nature of the individual while also representing their lucrative trades.

*Third Pada*

The third pada is in the Libra Navamsa and is governed by Venus. This phase is representative of the creativity that Venus grants, and the emphasis is on developing peace and relaxing.

*Fourth Pada*

The fourth pada is in the Scorpio Navamsa, governed by Mars. In this pada, the emphasis lands on emotional control. Typically, there is an emphasis on family life and introspection while also bolstering courage.

# Uttara Phalguni

Astronomical name: Beta Leonis
Deity: Aryaman
Lord: Sun
Color: Bright blue
Gemstone: Ruby

*Male characteristics*

Men born under this sign live lives full of joy and happiness. They are lucky individuals, but despite that, they are dedicated workers and remain neat and organized. Spiritual and leans toward community service. Though generally good-natured, they can also be hot-tempered. He can be impatient and intolerant, leading him to regret things done or said in anger.

*Female characteristics*

Calm and collected, women of this Nakshatra are happy-go-lucky and simplistic. They do not tend to create enemies. On the off chance they do, however, their rivals will change their tune after observing her sincere and pure nature.

*First Pada*

The first pada is in the Sagittarius Navamsa, governed by Jupiter. This phase emphasizes ethics, with the individual searching for or doing well as a consultant.

*Second Pada*

The second pada is in the Capricorn Navamsa, governed by Saturn. The emphasis is organizational skills, with desired outcomes sure to happen as a result.

*Third Pada*

The third pada is in the Aquarius Navamsa, governed by Saturn. Emphasis is on charity for others by making intelligent use of intellectual and financial resources.

*Fourth Pada*

The fourth pada is in the Pisces Navamsa, governed by Jupiter. Emphasis is on seeing the big picture and finding balance in it all.

# Hasta

*Astronomical name: Delta Corvi*
*Deity: Aditya*
*Lord: Moon*
*Color: Deep green*
*Gemstone: Natural Pearl*


*Male characteristics*

Male natives are calm and level-headed. His charm garners him attention from women. His temperament has a positive impact on those around him, which grants him respect. He is altruistic and willing to help those in need. Even if he ever accumulates wealth, he will not wish to flaunt his financial situation and instead prefers to live a quiet, simple life. Despite these qualities, he receives much criticism.

*Female characteristics*

Female natives are outspoken individuals that do not like being bossed around. The family may not appreciate her behavior, but she does have great respect for elders. Despite these qualities, she will work to maintain the household financially if needed or will gladly raise her children.

*First Pada*

The first pada is in the Aries Navamsa, governed by Mars. Emphasis on an abundance of energy as well as making the native knowledgeable about questionable activities.

*Second Pada*

The second pada is in the Taurus Navamsa, governed by Venus. Emphasis on enjoying the material and practicality. Natives are more honest than others.

*Third Pada*

The third pada is in the Gemini Navamsa, governed by Mercury. Emphasis on intellect and wit. Natives make good businessmen and professionals.

*Fourth Pada*

The fourth pada is in the Cancer Navamsa, governed by the moon. Emphasis familial and harmony and marital security.

# Chitra

*Astronomical name: Spica Virginis-Vegus*
*Deity: Tvashtav*
*Lord: Mars*
*Color: Black*
*Gemstone: Red Coral*

*Male characteristics*

Male natives are incredibly intelligent and opportunistic. Intuition is strong in these men, allowing them to come to conclusions quicker and better success than their peers. People may not understand the man's ideas at first, but eventually, they realize he was thinking many steps ahead and was ultimately right.

*Female characteristics*

Females in this Nakshatra are forward and crave an excess of freedom. This creates problems for her as it leads to a few friends and overindulgence in sinful behavior.

*First Pada*

The first pada is in the Leo Navamsa, governed by the Sun. Emphasis on self-reflection and trying to put thoughts into practice in their lives. Pride needs to be kept in check for behaviors to be positive, or they may come selfishly.

*Second Pada*

The second pada is in the Virgo Navamsa, governed by Mercury. Emphasis is on self-discipline, learning to be more discerning in their choices and behaviors, and engaging in groups.

*Third Pada*

The third pada is in the Libra Navamsa, governed by Venus. Emphasis is on arts and music. Associated with undoing positive work and unnecessary spending.

*Fourth Pada*

The fourth pada is in the Scorpio Navamsa, governed by Mars. Natives will pursue their ambitions with the prevalence of energy found here. Natives need to be mindful to utilize this energy for positive behavior.

# Swati

*Astronomical name: Arcturus*
*Deity: Vayu*
*Lord: Rahu*
*Color: Black*
*Gemstone: Gomedh*

*Male characteristics*

Natives are peaceful and independent. Works hard and despises cheats of call kinds. He is not short-tempered but is difficult to control when he does become angry. He is willing to help the needy, but not at the cost of his independence.

*Female characteristics*

She is compassionate and is respected by others. Honest and pure of heart, she is chaste, religious, and will dutifully perform her daily rituals that her family requires. She prefers to stay home as opposed to traveling. However, she does have an easy time making friends.

*First Pada*

The first pada is in the Sagittarius Navamsa, governed by Jupiter. Emphasis is on inquisitiveness and overcoming restlessness.

*Second Pada*

The second pada is in the Capricorn Navamsa, governed by Saturn. Emphasis on materialism while being grounded.

*Third Pada*

The third pada is in the Aquarius Navamsa, governed by Saturn. Emphasis on knowledge, creativity, team building to reach goals.

*Fourth Pada*

The fourth pada is in the Pisces Navamsa, governed by Jupiter. Emphasis on flexibility and following the tides, not swimming upstream.

# Vishakha

*Astronomical name: Alpha Librae*
*Deity: Indra-Agni*
*Lord: Jupiter*
*Color: Golden*
*Gemstone: Yellow sapphire*

*Male characteristics*

Males are intelligent and full of energy. Prioritizes truth and honesty. Hates superstitions but is a religious individual. Prefers to be progressive as opposed to holding conservative values.

*Female characteristics*

Female natives are charming due to their soft-spoken and sweet nature. She works well, domestically and at work. Like the male native, she is very religious. Possesses natural beauty that makes others jealous.

*First Pada*

The first pada is in the Aries Navamsa, governed by Mars. Emphasis on relationships. Provides energy and ambition.

*Second Pada*

The second pada is in the Taurus Navamsa, governed by Venus. Emphasis on endurance and durability. Natives are likely to be successful.

*Third Pada*

The third pada is in the Gemini Navamsa, governed by Mercury. Emphasis on having a one-track mind, which leads to natives achieving their goals.

*Fourth Pada*

The fourth pada is in the Cancer Navamsa, governed by the Moon. Emphasis is on overcoming emotional turmoil.

# Anuradha

*Astronomical name: Delta Scorpio*
*Deity: Mitra*
*Lord: Saturn*
*Color: Reddish brown*
*Gemstone: Blue sapphire*

*Male characteristics*

Male natives are typically handsome but may, on occasion, be the exact opposite. Systematically handles difficult situations. He is very hardworking but is vindictive and may lack peace of mind.

*Female characteristics*

Females have fantastic waists and innocent-looking faces, making them attractive to men. She prefers a simple life and does not pursue fashion or act with arrogance. Pure of heart, she is selfless and easy to get along with. She does well socially, and her circle of friends will protect her.

*First Pada*

The first pada is in the Leo Navamsa. Emphasis on self-reflection and applying what is learned into a career. Pride needs to be kept in check with positive thinking. Much energy shines through the Sun, Ketu, Jupiter, and Mars.

*Second Pada*

The second pada is in the Virgo Navamsa. Emphasis on discipline, learning, and working in groups. One can meet their ambitions in this pada.

*Third Pada*

The third pada is in the Libra Navamsa. Emphasis on the exotic, arts, and music. Natives are considered quite amiable.

*Fourth Pada*

The fourth pada is in the Scorpio Navamsa. Natives must be mindful of channeling excess energy positively.

# Jyeshtha

*Astronomical name: Antares*
*Deity: Indra*
*Lord: Mercury*
*Color: Cream*
*Gemstone: Emerald*

*Male characteristics*

The native is pure-minded. They cannot keep secrets to themselves and have a burning desire to remain open at all times. Male natives are stubborn and quick-tempered, leading to issues in life. This stubbornness also manifests with him not taking advice.

*Female characteristics*

Female natives are too sensitive and tend to get jealous. However, this is due to her love running deep. She always wants to know others' opinions of her. She is thoughtful, intuitive, and manages her household in an organized manner.

*First Pada*

The first pada is in the Sagittarius Navamsa, governed by Jupiter. Emphasis on finances, higher education, and generosity.

*Second Pada*

The second pada is in the Capricorn Navamsa, governed by Saturn. Emphasis is on integrity and doing the right thing, not the easy thing. To achieve goals, natives will need to work hard.

*Third Pada*

The third pada is in the Aquarius Navamsa, governed by Saturn. Emphasis is on the needs of others and being able to assist them. They need to be mindful so they do not get involved in strange sexual encounters.

*Fourth Pada*

The fourth pada is in the Pisces Navamsa, governed by Jupiter. Emphasis is on children, emotions, and exploring the exotic.

# Mula

*Astronomical name: Lambda Scorpio*
*Deity: Nirrti*
*Lord: Ketu*
*Color: Brownish yellow*
*Gemstone: Cat's eye*

*Male characteristics*

The male native is friendly and prefers peaceful environments. He is an optimistic person due to trust in God. He lives by his own values. Sometimes he may be vulnerable but is able to get over hurdles through willpower.

*Female characteristics*

The female native is pure of heart but stubborn. This stubbornness manifests even in petty things, which reflects poorly of her and can cause problems.

*First Pada*

The first pada is in the Aries Navamsa, governed by Mars. Emphasis on spiritual and material goals.

*Second Pada*

The second pada is in the Taurus Navamsa, governed by Venus. Emphasis is on the occult. Natives work hard and will reach their goals materially.

*Third Pada*

The third pada is in the Gemini Navamsa, governed by Mercury. Natives make great use of wordplay, which helps them communicate effectively.

*Fourth Pada*

The fourth pada is in the Cancer Navamsa, governed by the Moon. Emphasis is on empathy and trying to connect with people emotionally.

## Purva Ashadha

*Astronomical name: Delta Sagittarii*
*Deity: Jal*
*Lord: Venus*
*Color: Black*
*Gemstone: Diamond*

*Male characteristics*

Natives are intelligent but can be argumentative and impulsive. Always willing to give advice but has a hard time taking it. May have a courageous front but is not able to back it up on most occasions.

*Female characteristics*

The female native is intelligent and is full of energy. As a result, she is ambitious, with a desire to be the best in her chosen career. She perseveres through tough situations. She may over promise and not keep them all.

*First Pada*

The first pada is in the Leo Navamsa, governed by the Sun. Emphasis is self-confidence and pride. Natives like to be the center of attention.

*Second Pada*

The second pada is in the Virgo Navamsa, governed by Mercury. The native needs to put great effort into earning their money, but if they persist, they will be rewarded.

*Third Pada*

The third pada is in the Libra Navamsa, governed by Venus. The native is relaxed and enjoys material comforts. During this pada, natives reap what they have sown.

*Fourth Pada*

The fourth pada is in the Scorpio Navamsa, governed by Mars. Natives are arrogant, secretive, and mysterious. They will learn much occult wisdom.

# Uttara Ashadha

*Astronomical name: Sigma sagittari*
*Deity: Vishwa deva*
*Lord: Sun*
*Color: Copper*
*Gemstone: Ruby*

*Male characteristics*

Natives are soft-spoken, innocent, and pure of heart. Even if he were to reach great success in his career, his demeanor would not allow him to show off or behave arrogantly. Despite this, he may feel depressed if he does not receive recognition for his hard work.

*Female characteristics*

Natives are stubborn and prone to aggression. Despite this, they are uncomplicated individuals that like to keep things simple.

*First Pada*

The first pada is in the Sagittarius Navamsa, governed by Jupiter. Emphasis on growing self-confidence. Natives will gain much knowledge.

*Second Pada*

The second pada is in the Capricorn Navamsa, governed by Saturn. Emphasis on developing strategies to reach goals and desires.

*Third Pada*

The third pada is in the Aquarius Navamsa, governed by Saturn. Emphasis is on building up a wealth of knowledge and acquiring items that bring comfort.

*Fourth Pada*

The fourth pada is in the Pisces Navamsa, governed by Jupiter. Emphasis will shift between the material and the spiritual.

# Shravana

*Astronomical name: Alpha Aquilae*
*Deity: Vishnu*
*Lord: Moon*
*Color: Light blue*
*Gemstone: Natural pearl*

*Male characteristics*

Male natives are methodical in their work. He has a set of values that he lives by, such as cleanliness and maintaining his environment in an orderly manner. While he seeks to help the needy, he will be backstabbed by those he helps. Tends to hit the mid-level in his career.

*Female characteristics*

Female natives are charitable and religious. Despite this, she likes to show off her charity so that others are aware of her acts. She is very chatty and cannot hide anything from her husband.

*First Pada*

The first pada is in the Aries Navamsa, governed by Mars. Natives will seek to build up logic, initiative, and ambition.

*Second Pada*

The second pada is in the Taurus Navamsa, governed by Venus. Natives behave in a diplomatic fashion. Emphasis is on music and entertainment.

*Third Pada*

The third pada is in the Gemini Navamsa, governed by Mercury. Natives will emphasize communication and a desire to gain knowledge.

*Fourth Pada*

The fourth pada is in the Cancer Navamsa, governed by the Moon. Emphasis is on sympathy and being receptive to others. Natives may hold public offices or work in hospitality.

# Danishtha

Astronomical name: Beta Delphinium
Deity: Ashta vasav
Lord: Mars

# Manjula Tara

Color: Silver-grey
Gemstone: Red coral

## Male characteristics

Natives are intelligent and experts of their craft. They hate doing anything that may cause problems for others. Despite this, natives are vindictive. They are patient individuals, so they are willing to wait until the time is right to get their revenge.

## Female characteristics

Females are ambitious and tend to spend their money frivolously. Despite this, they tend to be humble and show much compassion for the poor. She may have a domineering personality but needs to hold back for the good of her family.

## First Pada

The first pada is in the Leo Navamsa, governed by the Sun. With the Sun, Mars, and Saturn, the emphasis is on material achievement. The native will be successful in all areas but marriage.

## Second Pada

The second pada is in the Virgo Navamsa, governed by Mercury. The native is an excellent communicator. Marriage is still a problem, but skills in sports and music shine.

## Third Pada

The third pada is in the Libra Navamsa, governed by Venus. Natives are happy-go-lucky and are successful in marriage. Natives excel in spirituality, astrology, and performance arts.

*Fourth Pada*

The fourth pada is in the Scorpio Navamsa, governed by Mars. Natives will do well in outdoor sports and high-intensity physical activities. Natives will seek to care for the needy but may face problems at home.

# Shatabhisha

*Astronomical name: Lambda Aquarius*
*Deity: Varuna*
*Lord: Rahu*
*Color: Aquamarine*
*Gemstone: Gomedh*

*Male characteristics*

Male natives tend to self-sacrifice interests in favor of their principles. They tend to follow their rituals carefully and strictly and are stubborn as well. They are quite intelligent and also somewhat emotional.

*Female characteristics*

The female native is likely to be very calm, but when provoked, it can be really problematic. They can develop high tempers when they are provoked. She is likely to care about religion and tends to get into fights with her families as well. Mental peace is hard for her to come across in her life. She is known to have a good memory and is usually quite generous and sympathetic.

*First Pada*

This pada is in the Sagittarius Navamsa and is ruled by Jupiter. This native is usually quite casual while also possessing plenty of optimism and may also get cheated often as well.

*Second Pada*

The second pada is in the Capricorn Navamsa by Saturn. It is very practical and even methodical at times. She may tend toward being too ambitious sometimes as well.

*Third Pada*

The third pada is known to be in the Aquarius Navamsa, ruled by Saturn. This individual is likely to be eccentric and even aggressive sometimes as well.

*Fourth Pada*

The fourth pada is in the Pisces Navamsa in Jupiter. This creates a compassionate individual with an emphasis on healing. This native may have an addictive personality.

## Purva Bhadrapada

*Astronomical name: Alpha Pegasi*
*Deity: Ajaikapada*
*Lord: Jupiter*
*Color: Silver grey*
*Gemstone: Yellow sapphire*

*Male characteristics*

This native tends to be very peace-loving, but they may have a bit of a temper sometimes as well. He is likely to live a simple life. With strict values adhered to, he is likely to suffer if he sees them counteracted. When he is speaking to groups, he tends to be impartial to all. He refuses to blindly believe in things, religious or otherwise. He loves to help the needy but is hated anyway.

*Female characteristics*

The female native is likely, to be honest at work. She is likely to stick to her principles as much as possible and thrives in leadership situations. She is easy to work with others to work smoothly as well, which creates success for her.

*First Pada*

The first pada falls in the Aries Navamsa, under Mars. These natives are typically more aggressive, mentally typically more so than physically. They tend to be controlling and aggressive but still manage to achieve their goals no matter what.

*Second Pada*

The second pada is ruled by Taurus, controlled by Venus. The focus here is an indulgence. These natives tend to be very energetic and typically express the dark side of their personality.

*Third Pada*

The third pada is in Gemini, ruled by Mercury. The emphasis here is on creating strong communication skills, and the native is typically very curious and even humorous sometimes.

*Fourth Pada*

The fourth pada is in the Cancer Navamsa, ruled by the Moon. This placement creates a focus on being capable of persecuting.

## Uttara Bhadrapada

*Astronomical name: Gamma Pegasi*

*Deity: Ahir Budhnya*
*Lord: Saturn*
*Color: Purple*
*Gemstone: Blue sapphire*

*Male characteristics*

This individual tends to avoid discrimination as much as possible. They enjoy people as friends, with little regard for caste. They tend to work well, and they have pure hearts, but they also tend to be quite temperamental as well. They usually do not last much in these connections. He possesses plenty of knowledge, as well.

*Female characteristics*

Females born under this combination tend to be wealthy. She is usually very well-respected and behaves well as well. She is likely to be very successful in just about any circumstances, thanks to her adaptability. She is known for being impartial and always fighting for justice.

*First Pada*

This is in the Leo Navamsa ruled by the Sun. The natives here are typically very proud and goal-oriented. They are very knowledgeable and emphasize spreading experience.

*Second Pada*

The second pada is in the Virgo Navamsa, ruled by Mercury. It creates an emphasis on planning and analysis. These individuals generally get to do a lot of back-end work and thrive.

*Third Pada*

The third pada is in the Libra Navamsa that is ruled by Venus. This combination creates a native who is balanced and grounded. Their orientation is usually very objective.

*Fourth Pada*

The fourth pada is in the Scorpio Navamsa, ruled by Mars. Here, the emphasis is on creating an individual that is mysterious and wise.

## Revati

*Astronomical name: Zeta Piscum*
*Deity: Pooshvav*
*Lord: Mercury*
*Color: Brown*
*Gemstone: Emerald*

*Male characteristics*

This native is likely to be very kind, soft-spoken, and pure at heart. They tend to be very sincere and honest as well with people they know and with people around them. They tend to be unlikely to hurt other people with their words or deeds and prefer to be independent. They can be hurt when people try to control them, and they will not trust blindly. They get attached regularly, and when they are held back, they can struggle with depression.

*Female characteristics*

Females in this placement tend to be very stubborn and even domineering sometimes. They dominate their professional and personal lives, but despite this, they also tend to be very religious as well.

*First Pada*

The first pada is in the Sagittarius sign, ruled by Jupiter. These individuals tend to be very generous and even casual at times. They are typically quite optimistic.

*Second Pada*

The second pada is in the Capricorn Navamsa under Saturn. These individuals are usually quite organized and stick to popular paths rather than attempting to take risks.

*Third Pada*

The third pada is in the Aquarius Navamsa, also ruled by Saturn. These individuals are usually compassionate and empathetic, as well. They love to help other people.

*Fourth Pada*

The fourth pada is in the Pisces Navamsa that is lorded by Jupiter. These natives usually find themselves as big daydreamers. They are very easy to influence.

## Introducing the Yogas

In Vedic Astrology, there are certain combinations that are referred to as yogas. The yogas are combinations on your chart to create certain patterns. Together, when you take the patterns, you start seeing the characteristics that you are looking for. Through looking at how the various Planets align themselves, you can then start piecing together information about the person.

Yogas become an incredibly important part of reading your chart thanks to the fact that they will have very different meanings. They add more depth to your chart and allow you to understand more based upon the placements. Some are auspicious while others are inauspicious, and as you get to know them and what they mean, you will start gaining the abilities that you will need to better read people around you.

The next portion of this chapter is going to have you specifically looking at the most commonly acknowledged yogas in your chart. They will help you to start understanding more about your own horoscope and will help you to get more context to what is happening. We are going to take a look at several combinations to get an understanding of what they are and what they mean for you here. We will start by going over the most important yogas for you to know, followed by those that are deemed auspicious. From there, we will go over inauspicious yogas, and finally, those involving the Sun and the moon.

## A Note on the Kendras

Before we delve into those yogas, however, it is important for you to know what the Kendras are. The Kendra houses are the auspicious houses that are on your chart. These are the first, fourth, seventh, and tenth houses on a natal chart. These Planets are the ones that will create health, wealth, and intelligence. The Kendras are the houses of Vishnu, and Lord Vishnu is believed to be connected to stability, savings, and security.

Auspicious Planets within the Kendras give positive results. Their good health and other blessings can create good luck overall in marriage and in professional lives. Each of the Kendra houses become crucial to reading the Yogas because of how they influence your chart. Generally speaking, the more Planets found in the Kendra houses, the more auspicious the reading. Within the four houses, they vary in luck. The most auspicious house is the 10$^{th}$ House. Then, the 7$^{th}$ is the second most auspicious. From there, the 4$^{th}$ House is the third most auspicious, and the 1$^{st}$ House is the least auspicious. However, all four are still considered to be auspicious. Each house will have its own effects.

*The 1st House (1st Kendra House)*

The first Kendra House is the Ascendant. This is reminiscent of the beginning of childhood, health, individuality, and the surrounding aspects of life. This is indicative of the strength of the horoscope in general.

*The 4th House (2nd Kendra House)*

This house represents the Home, internal happiness, and the happiness of the mother. It is good for looking at properties such as intelligence.

*The 7th House (3rd Kendra House)*

This house is recognized as being representative of marriage, spouses, happiness in marriage, and the like. It can also help to identify travel and friendships.

*The 10th House (4th Kendra House)*

This house is the most important and will help to influence the ability and competency of the individual. This Kendra is important to judge the complexity of a person, as well as the religion and success of them.

## Important Yogas

The yogas listed here are very powerful and generally quite rare. However, their effects are strong and create massive changes to the individual. You may not ever see these particular yogas, or you may see them very rarely, but they are important to know.

### Gaja Kesari-Yoga

This yoga is created by the placement of both Jupiter and the Moon. It is considered to be an auspicious yoga and is quite desirable. To get this yoga, you will see an angle between Jupiter and the Moon. In particular, you will see this happen in 1st, 4th, 7th, and 10th places. This yoga will grant the individual good luck, wealth, children, and general prosperity and knowledge.

Jupiter should be in its own sign, or in a sign of a friend planet, and when it gets a benefic aspect, such as Mercury or Venus, it becomes more powerful. This yoga will also help to protect a person and sort of balance out the adverse effect of other Planets that may be causing issues.

**Kedar Yoga**

This yoga is quite simple to spot—you will see all seven Planets present in the four houses on your birth chart. This combination is quite rare, but it is also quite beneficial to the individual. You will see that with this combination, the native is likely to be quite charitable and earns a lot of fame and income with how they work. They work hard and tend to lean toward working the land, such as in farming.

**Kahal Yoga**

This yoga is created when the lords of the 9th and 4th houses present themselves in mutual angles, with the lord of the Ascendant strong. It also requires the lord of the 4th to be in an exaltation state or in their own sign with an aspect of the 10th lord. This yoga can be a bit contradictory but is quite special for the native.

The one who is lucky enough to have the Kahala yoga will tend to be quite noble and radiant as a person. They are going to be very well-loved, and their personality is enough to radiate positivity and confidence. These natives tend to be very well-versed and can command armies and cities with ease. This person will be kind and noble. However, they may also be somewhat foolish at times. They must struggle to achieve the success that they can reach.

## Kamal Yoga

This yoga is created when all Planets are placed into the 1st, 4th, 7th, and 10th houses of the birth chart. When all Planets align in this manner, the individual is said to have a good chance at success. This is a very rare yoga, but it is quite positive. This native will show that they have a wonderful, radiant personality and will be blessed with a long life with a good heart to go with it. You may become famous as you achieve your goals, and you will get everything that you could ever dream of.

## Musala Yoga

Musala Yoga is created when all Planets are present in the fixed signs (remember, the fixed signs are Taurus, Leo, Scorpio, and Aquarius). This allows this person to pick up their steadfast nature from those signs, and this native is going to be driven toward their hard work.

Those born under the Musala Yoga are those who are going to be reliable and are driven toward fame and achievements. They tend to excel administratively and will find themselves accumulating wealth and benefits.

## Neechabhanga Raja Yoga

The last of the special yogas that we will look at is the Neechabhanga Raja Yoga. Its name combines "Neecha," meaning debilitated, and "bhanga," meaning annulled. This one is a combination that allows for the ill effects of a debilitated planet to be canceled out. This allows for the individual to attain high status, full of authority and comfort. To achieve this yoga, several criteria need to be met. However, if they are met, this is one of the most powerful yogas there are.

First, the debilitated planet must be in the angle from the Moon or from the Ascendant. Then, the Lord of the sign that is debilitating the planet must be in the center from the ascendant or from the Moon.

The exalted planet of the sign that the debilitated planet is in should be angled from the ascendant or moon. The Lord of a sign must impact the debilitated planet of the same sign. The Lord of the planet that is debilitated and the Lord of the planet that is exalted must both be in the center from the Moo nor the Ascendant. The Lord of the debilitated sign and the Lord of the exalted sign must be in the center from the ascendant.

## Auspicious Yogas

These yogas are also very important to know. They are powerful and special, creating the effects of positivity and auspicious luck on those with them in their charts. If you want to see these positive results, you will take a look at the following yoga patterns.

### Ruchaka Yoga

The Ruchaka Yoga is created when Mars is in the Capricorn sign (exalting it), or in its own sign (Aries or Scorpio) and is in angle from the Ascendant or from the Moon. Mars is indicative of power and physical prowess, and as such, you will see this yoga enhancing those traits. In particular, the individual will be brave, strong, and intelligent. He will be known for being able to overcome his enemies and adversity and may be either a warrior or an athlete as a result.

## Bhadra Yoga

On the charts, the Bhadra Yoga is created when Mercury is in its own sign (Either Gemini or Virgo) or is in its exaltation sign and at the same time is in the Kendra house from the Ascendant or from the Moon. These natives tend to attain fame thanks to the positive traits that they tend to show. Through developing those skills of communication and their need for perfection, they are very successful.

The Bhadra Yoga draws its name from the word "Bhadra," meaning gentleman. This yoga creates someone who will have a gentle disposition. Mercury is involved in this particular formation and implies that the native will be intelligent, have a strong memory, and well-versed in learning. The benefic qualities of Mercury are particularly strong in this individual.

## Hansa Yoga

The Hansa Yoga is created by Jupiter being placed in its own sign, either Sagittarius or Pisces, or in exaltation in Cancer. Jupiter must also occupy a Kendra house from the Ascendant or Moon. When Jupiter is placed well in the chart, it will create strong effects that create auspicious results.

This formation is known to create people who are religious, intelligent, knowledgeable, and very willing to help other people. This individual is expected to be happy, strong, and auspicious and is expected to have a long and happy life.

## Malavya Yoga

Malavya Yoga is a strong one involving Venus. This particular yoga creates the effect of making beautiful, cultured natives who are quite lucky and capable of success. They usually inherit the benefic qualities that you would expect to see with Venus. The native is likely to live long and have a prosperous life.

This particular yoga is formed when Venus is in its own sign, either Taurus or Libra, or is in exaltation in Pisces, and also occupies a Kendra house from the Ascendant or the Moon. Venus, when well-placed, will also create strong and beneficial results. life.

**Sasa Yoga**

The Sasa Yoga involves Saturn and will grant the native abundance in the land while also blessing them with the power of authority. The benefic qualities of Saturn are inherited by the native, and as a result, the individual gets a long life with happiness. Commonly, this yoga creates politicians and other natives who are going to have the power to lead people. He may be fickle and shrewd but is also known to be healthy and wealthy as well.

This yoga is created when Saturn is in its own sign (either Capricorn or Aquarius) or in its exaltation sign of Libra. It must also occupy the Kendra house either from the ascendant or from the Moon. When Saturn is placed well, there are stronger results.

## Inauspicious Yogas

So far, we have seen several yogas that are highly beneficial. However, there are also yogas that are difficult to manage as well. These yogas that you will see here are considered harmful yogas that are likely to cause all sorts of issues for the natives under these signs. These yogas are, in a lot of ways, incredibly important to know and understand because they can cause serious strife for the person born under them. Keep an eye out for these six yogas when reading charts.

**Kemdrum Yoga**

Kemdrum Yoga is one that is highly negative. In fact, it is one of the worst yogas that you can have unless it is canceled out by the placement or aspect of another benefic planet that is present in a chart. This is created when the 2nd and 12th houses have no Planets but the Sun, Rahu, and Ketu. This yoga is known to create poverty, failure, and struggles. This is because the Moon, which is the most important planet on your chart, gets no support from any others. It is alone, and that causes the person born under this yoga to lack any blessing from the moon.

However, when the Moon has the aspect of benefic planets, the effects of the Kemdrum Yoga are weakened significantly. This can also happen if there is a positive or benefic planet placed in the Kendra from Moon or Ascendant.

**Daridra Yoga**

Daridra Yoga is one that is also bad for the people. It is created when the lord of the eleventh house is in the sixth, eighth, or twelfth house of the birth chart. If the lords of the 11th, 9th, or 2nd house have connections with the sixth, eighth, or twelfth house, the Daridra Yoga may also form. This yoga is one that causes hardships or difficulties in life.

**Grahan Yoga**

The Grahan Yoga is created when the Sun and Moon, also known as luminaries, are impacted by Rahu and Ketu. The Sun is representative of the soul, while the Moon is representative of the mind. When they are impacted by Rahu and Ketu, the individual is likely to find themselves or herself lacking stability. They are likely to be restless throughout life because of the afflicted Sun or Moon in their life.

**Shakat Yoga**

The Shakat Yoga is also malefic. In this yoga, you will find Jupiter in the sixth or eighth house from the Moon. Though Jupiter is a benefic planet, when it is in the sixth or eighth house from the Moon, it is considered bad. The position leads to a person who is unhappy in life, arrogant in nature, and likely to find all sorts of obstructions in marriage.

### Chandal Yoga

This yoga is negative, forming when Jupiter is combusted with Rahu. When combined, the native is likely to lose the benefic nature of Jupiter. So while Jupiter may be a prosperous sign, when a part of the Chandal Yoga, it is actually problematic.

### Kuja Yoga

Finally, let's look at Kuja Yoga. This is created when Mars is in houses 1, 4, 7, 8, or 12. When this happens, it is sometimes called the Mangalik Dosha. It negatively impacts married life.

## Yogas of the Sun

Some yogas are formed by the sun. The yogas of the Sun create influences over the people in many different ways, but there are three in particular that we are going to address. These three yogas are incredibly powerful in their own ways, and they will involve the placement of the sun.

### Veshi Yoga

Veshi Yoga is created when there are planets, other than the Moon or Rahu and Ketu, in the second house from the sun. However, the result of the yoga is dependent on the presence of the Planets that are present. If the second house has benefic Planets in it, there will be positive and desirable results related to that planet, while malefic Planets will create negative results.

The benefits placed in this yoga will create religious individuals. They will be honest and happy and thought there would be some challenges; sometimes, he is likely to overcome them over time. The malefic Planets also create effects that will be present. In particular, there will be difficulties that are challenging to get past.

## Vaasi Yoga

Vaasi Yoga is created when there is a planet, other than the Moon or Rahu and Ketu, in the 12th house from the Sun. However, the result will be dependent upon the nature of the planet in the house. As with the Veshi Yoga, benefic Planets are going to be beneficial, while malefic Planets will create challenges. Typically, this yoga is related to the spiritual tendencies of an individual, and that will create people who are noble. They will create people who are hardworking and intelligent, as well as kind and charitable. He is likely to be successful in governmental positions if he has a benefic planet in this position.

## Ubhayachari Yoga

The Ubhayachari Yoga is created when there is a planet on either side of the Sun, aside from the Moon or Rahu and Ketu. When you have the Veshi and the Vaasi yoga at the same time, you get the Ubhayachari Yoga. This person is known to be very well behaved and typically quite resourceful as well. If there are benefic Planets in this yoga, the individual is likely to be courageous and have a good circle of friends. The Malefic Planets in this route, however, will reduce the effect.

## Yogas of the Moon

There are also yogas of the Moon that must be considered as well. These are yogas that will directly relate to the Moon somehow. Remember, the Moon is incredibly important in your reading. You want to make sure that you learn these four yogas and start applying them to your readings of charts as well.

**Sunafa Yoga**

The first yoga that we are going to look at is Sunafa Yoga. This is created when there are planets, other than the Sun or Rahu and Ketu, in the second house from the moon. This is auspicious and will create good luck, prosperity, intelligence, wealth, positivity, and happiness for the native. The native is likely to be self-made and is able to get anything that he wants in the world.

If there are benefits to this Yoga, then it is a good chance that the individual is going to see stronger results. However, if there are malefic Planets playing a part in this yoga, the result is going to drain the auspicious yoga.

**Anafa Yoga**

The Anafa Yoga is created when there are Planets in the twelfth house from the Moon. This is also an auspicious Yoga and creates positive qualities for the native. The native is likely to be healthy while also being quite attractive to others. He is likely to be famous, or at the very least, respected, and that allows him to gain support from others. He is usually very patient and happy in life. Mars, in particular in this Yoga, is highly beneficial and gives leadership and strength. Mercury also makes him skilled in being good at communication. Jupiter makes the native religious, knowledgeable, and involved in charitable actions. Venus creates other effects, causing someone to focus on sexual actions. Saturn, on the other hand, can create problems.

**Durudhara Yoga**

Durudhara Yoga is created when you have Planets on either side of the Moon, with the exception of the Moon and Rahu and Ketu. You can actually get this effect as well if you have both the Sunafa and the Anafa yogas. This is a good, auspicious formation and is going to create a native who is comfortable and living happily thanks to his work. He is likely to be famous and is more likely than not to be trustworthy and intelligent. The end result is that this person is going to be very kind. He is likely to have a strong benefic effect, and that makes him a great person to be around. On the other hand, malefics in houses can cause other issues. From the effects of womanizing to being cruel to others or greedy, a malefic in this yoga is negative.

**Kema Druma Yoga**

Kema Druma Yoga is created when there is no planet on either side of the Moon. The end result is that the Moon does not get any support at all. The Moon then becomes weak, and as a result, the native end up living a lonely life that is difficult and unsatisfied. This is a huge problem for him. It can cause the individual to be miserable. There are some effects that can actually start to combat the negativity, however. These include:

- The Moon in Kendra or trikona from the Ascendant
- The Moon in conjunction with other Planets in the house that it is situated
- The Moon has an aspect of the planets. The benefic planet is usually stronger.

# Planets in Constellations

## Sun

The Sun is one of the most important parts of Vedic astrology. As the center of the solar system, the Sun may be entirely still, but because of how the Earth rotates and revolves around the Sun, the Sun appears to travel through the constellations nonetheless.

# Reading Your Chart in the Sky

Looking at the Sun will help you to understand more about yourself. It is the giver of life, and when you read it in astrology, you are answering questions about who you are. You are taking a look at the reasons for what you do. It is creative and strong. The Sun will tell you what you are to do in the world as well as your personality. Depending on where your Sun sign is, you will see very different results.

## Sun in Aries

Aries is ruled by Mars, which, like the Sun, is fierce and masculine. However, because the Sun and Mars both share a friendly relationship, the Sun in Aries also creates good results as well. This person is going to be strong and capable—he or she is likely to be a guiding leader and a force to be reckoned with. He will show a strong sense of responsibility and be smart, strong, and also very prosperous. However, he may also show signs of aggressiveness from time to time.

## Sun in Taurus

Taurus is ruled by Venus and is a fixed earth sign. However, Venus is feminine and watery, while the Sun is masculine and fiery. The result is that they are doubly inimical to each other, meaning that they do not work well together. The Sun in Taurus, then, becomes a very malefic combination. Natives born with the Sun in Taurus tend to struggle a lot in life, facing all sorts of challenges. Their physical health tends to be lacking as well—they are likely to struggle with their immune system and may be vulnerable to issues with the eyes and face. Water may also be dangerous to this person as well. They are also likely to struggle in marriage with their unfavorable sign for marriage.

Despite this, however, those in this sign also find that they are blessed with good looks, humility, and intelligence. They tend to thrive in artistic endeavors and can also earn plenty of wealth as well.

## Sun in Gemini

Gemini is an air sign lorded by Mercury, which is neutral and earthy. Because the Sun and Mercury are friends, they have a neutral relationship, and that means that the Sun in Gemini is neutral, skewing slightly to the positive side. This person is likely to be quite intelligent and is able to hold their own in debating as well. With the Sun in Gemini, you will see that the native is generally quite logical and is skilled in many fields. They thrive working in the financial sector or as accountants. They are great at communicating with others and are skilled at persuasion as well. Natives with this placement also tend to be great at judging others, but also make sure to avoid using them for their own benefit. Typically, they are interested in space and thrive in sciences as well. They work hard, and sometimes harder than average, to meet their goals, and that can be distressing, but by and large, this is a positive arrangement.

## Sun in Cancer

Cancer represents a movable water sign that is lorded over by the Moon. The Moon is feminine and watery, as well. Despite the fact that the fiery and masculine nature of the Sun is contradictory with the watery feminine side of the Moon, they actually do share a friendly relationship together. They balance each other out. They create a balance between the masculine and the feminine, and that allows for stability in the individual. These natives are very virtuous, and they tend to follow a pious path. They will live according to their morals and will be primarily positive.

## Sun in Leo

Leo is a fixed fire sign that is ruled by the Sun. This means that the Sun in its own sign is the Sun in its own sign, and that is very good. When this placement is on your horoscope, then you are blessed by the positivity and benefic nature of the Sun. The Native is likely to win all of their competitions that they enter, and they have strong instincts that can be aggressive and even selfish at times, but those instincts do lead them in the right direction. This particular combination is very important. It allows the individual to be strong and have the power to be revolutionary as well. They will work tirelessly to get to the end that they want and are particularly well suited to be in the government.

*Sun in Virgo*

Virgo is an Earth sign ruled by Mercury. Because of the fact that Mercury is friends with the Sun, and the Sun is neutral toward Mercury, the relationship is generally considered to be positive. Those with this placement tend to be very intelligent and able to learn well. They are typically able to calculate what is necessary and also communicate well as well. Typically, these people find themselves particularly skilled in debates, writing, and teaching. These natives also thrive in math, as well. Additionally, they are likely to be very creative and artistic, as well. They have logic and kindness, and yet still tend to be religious as well. This is generally considered largely positive.

*Sun in Libra*

Libra is an air sign that resides in the feminine and water planet of Venus. The Sun, on the other hand, is considered masculine and also fiery. Venus and the Sun are considered enemies for each other. The Sun is also debilitated in Libra as well. This is perhaps one of the worst positions for the Sun due to these factors that come into play. These make the Sun struggle and also be deemed problematic by authority figures. The native is likely to live a life that is full of difficulties and challenges. They may find that they are stuck with all sorts of unwanted expenses, or they may find that they are having issues with relationships as well. They are likely to suffer intense frustration and even devastation in life. They sometimes struggle in relationships and tend to become harsh and manipulative, or even immoral at times. They can get too self-involved and care only about themselves. This causes a lot of issues for them as well. They struggle in social settings or in relationships with people as a result.

*Sun in Scorpio*

Scorpio is fixed and watery, ruled by Mars. Mars and the Sun are both masculine fiery Planets that are quite friendly with each other. However, because Scorpio is also associated with the 8th house, it is not always positive. The 8th house relates to death and other negative experiences. Having the Sun in Scorpio creates a highly emotional person, with many emotions buried within themselves. They are highly emotional and yet still compassionate toward others as well. They are typically considered highly prone to lying and may also have a sense of unhappiness as well. They tend to be dissatisfied in life, as well as in their marriage, and they tend to engage in arguments as well. They typically also do not have a very good relationship with their parents either. They are typically found to be ambitious, however, and tend to truly respect themselves. They are cautious with money and tend to plan carefully.

*Sun in Sagittarius*

Sagittarius is a fire sign that is ruled by the fiery Jupiter. Jupiter and the Sun share a friendly relationship, and as a result, this creates a positive combination when the Sun enters Sagittarius. This native is likely to be god-fearing but peace-loving and will be quite skilled in speech. This native is likely to be quite intelligent and compassionate toward others. They yearn for as much knowledge as they can gain, and they work well in law as a result. These individuals are known for their focus on justice and trustworthiness, and they are very honest. They understand the difference between having a life and simply surviving—they love to spend time outdoors as well and tend to be very adept athletically. They are typically quite beautiful and enjoy plenty of support in their social lives.

## Sun in Capricorn

Capricorn represents a movable Earth sign that is ruled by Saturn, a planet that is known for its fearsome effects on others. Saturn is an airy planet and is inimical with the Sun. Though Saturn is largely regarded as malefic, it is not meant to only be a negative sign for you. Capricorn natives typically are bold and carefree. They are more or less combated by the Sun, and therefore the Sun's effect on the native is somewhat minimal. Due to this, these individuals tend to show many signs of their Moon sign. These natives tend to be very serious, responsible, and thoughtful. They are known for their patience, which they use to fend off the constant delays caused by Saturn. They work hard and continue on nonetheless. They are loyal and expect the same sort of loyalty from those close to them as well.

## Sun in Aquarius

Aquarius is an airy sign that is also ruled by Saturn. As we already reiterated, Saturn is inimical toward the Sun. Between that and the airy Aquarius fanning the Sun, this position is a relatively neutral one. The native will become short-tempered and may be extra frugal with their spending. They are typically quite eccentric but still manage to be liked by others. They tend to be very emotional and put their own needs on the back burner if they are able to aid others. They tend to pay more attention to society than individual people. They can be great in humanitarian positions and could be good leaders. They will tend to be honest and value their friends while also maintaining compassion and humility. Typically, however, they try to avoid showing their feelings to those around them.

## Sun in Pisces

Pisces is a water sign ruled by the watery Jupiter. Both Jupiter and the Sun are considered to be friendly, and because of that, the Sun in Pisces is actually a relatively positive one. Those with this sign placement tend to be very friendly in nature. These natives usually find that they are comfortable with servants, and usually, they work toward having a good spouse and great children. The male natives tend to be very fond of women, and they are typically very fond of traveling when possible. They usually find that they are quite happy and they build up wealth as well. Their intellect and intuition help them in basically all aspects of their lives.

However, there is a layer of moodiness in there as well. Sometimes, they struggle to understand themselves and become quite emotional as a result. They value the opinions of others, and though they are adaptable, they also sometimes veer toward throwing themselves into everything that they do, especially work. They are very ambitious, and they do everything in their power to throw themselves all into their projects. They want to be the best versions of themselves possible. They care a lot about themselves and their respect and status in society.

## Moon

The Moon is an incredibly important part of Vedic astrology as well. While the Sun represents the individual, the Moon represents emotion. It shows how your mental state is and what you are likely to do. The Sun is masculine, and the Moon is almost the opposite—

it is the feminine. It represents the mind and inner self. Those with prominent Moons on their horoscope tend to be highly emotional and nurturing, and especially those with Moon in Cancer tend to thrive as parents.

## Moon in Aries

Aries is ruled by Mars, a fiery and masculine planet. Though they clash, it is important to note that Mars is friendly with the Moon. This means that though there is this sort of conflict of energy, the native is likely to get some benefits from both sides. They may be aggressive at times but also find that they are quite honest and even resolute as well. This native allows their subconscious to manifest itself to make decisions without thinking much about it. There is a higher than average degree of self-respect here, and this creates a sort of restlessness and recklessness at the same time. This individual may be crabby at times but is largely self-motivated and willing to pursue what they want no matter what. They are quite active and enjoy the way that they live. They work on life by living one day at a time rather than trying to plan ahead, and they tend to do great with this.

## Moon in Taurus

Taurus is ruled by Venus, but the Moon in Taurus is a point of exaltation as well. However, Venus and the Moon share an enemy relationship. Due to their shared water element, however, their energy tends to balance out well, and those with Moon in Taurus tend to reap the benefits despite the rocky relationship between the Moon and Venus. These individuals tend to be attractive, romantic, and look great as well. They are charitable and very generous, and they tend to race to help those in need whenever possible.

These individuals tend to get great benefits from Venus and gain riches in life. They are usually happiest in the middle part of their lives, and they are quite grounded, but also big-hearted as well. They tend to be loyal and intelligent, and they usually make very fun of individuals who are drawn to the arts.

## Moon in Gemini

Gemini is ruled by Mercury, and due to the inimical relationship between the Moon and Mercury, this becomes a very difficult position. The Moon's feminine, watery nature is not very well suited to the neutral, earthy position of Mercury. However, this placement does allow for some good traits. The native is likely to be friendly and cheerful, but also emotional and reserved at the same time. They are likely to suffer in loneliness and will likely struggle to make good relationships. Likewise, they tend to be mentally sharp as well and are good at forming quick impressions that happen to be spot on as well. These natives are typically very social and love to have a huge social circle. They tend to get attached quickly, and communication is one of their strong points.

## Moon in Cancer

Cancer is ruled by the Moon, making the Moon quite comfortable in this position. This allows for some of the strongest influences of the Moon. If you have this placement, you are likely to be not only going to be driven but also determined and also accommodating at the same time. This native will be highly emotional and receptive to the feelings of others and will be strongly imaginative. However, the degree of sentimentality developed by this person can actually flaw them sometimes—it can make it difficult for the individual to get past those emotions. However, this individual also likes to hide their own feelings whenever possible. They are likely to deeply love their family, and they flourish as a parent. They tend to love romance and desire someone who is going to love them. Despite their peaceful nature, they can sometimes become crabby as well.

## Moon in Leo

Leo is a sign ruled by the fiery, masculine Sun, but despite that, remember that the Sun and Moon have a friendly relationship. They work together, balancing each other out. The Sun and Moon work similarly to the balance of the mother and father of a household, balancing each other out and providing aspects that would otherwise be lacking. When the fire of the Sun becomes too much, the watery Moon is there to start balancing it out. The Moon in Leo allows for this sort of balance to be managed as well. This native is likely to be confident and a strong leader. They rely on themselves more than they ask for help, and they tend to allow their emotions to sway them at times. They gain the confidence from Leo and still get the strength and compassion from the Moon, making them almost regal.

## Moon in Virgo

Virgo is recognized for its calculating nature. It is ruled by Mercury, which is also intellectual as well. Because the relationship between the Moon and Mercury is neutral, this position is relatively neutral as well. This native is likely to be attractive, skilled in communication, and very capable of being truthful and pure. They are commonly quite religious and find great pleasure in being compassionate to others. It is difficult to find a way to label them, and while they are not quite sentimental, they are also not unemotional. They have complex feelings that can be hard to navigate through. This individual may believe that they are inferior oftentimes, and they are driven more by their intellectual nature more than their instinctive one. Whatever they do is typically driven by logic and common sense. They tend to be highly practical and will accept reality for exactly what it is. They tend to help others that are needy and have a strong philosophical sense of themselves.

## Moon in Libra

Libra is ruled by Venus, the feminine watery planet. However, despite both Planets sharing those similarities, the two have an inimical relationship. This means that Libra and the Moon do not tend to get along very well. This can create a bit of conflict in the individual. Thanks to the dual nature of femininity that is created with this conversation, the individual tends to be generous and understanding, and even tolerant in many situations. There is also a degree of heightened interest in sex, thanks to the heightened passion and sensuality. This individual is known to be very emotional in nature. Though ambitious, this individual is likely to lean on other people, particularly women, and especially one's mother. This individual tends to be very sociable and enjoys lending helping hands when possible. The native is likely to be very accommodating and seeks justice whenever possible, preferring peace and pleasantries.

## Moon in Scorpio

Scorpio is ruled by Mars, a fiery and masculine planet. Additionally, the Moon is debilitated by Scorpio. Though Mars and the Moon enjoy a friendly relationship, it is important to recognize that debilitation. This is not a positive combination. This native is likely to be very frugal and is likely to not be very attractive either. The native may be mysterious but sometimes overly sensitive as well. They tend to be ruled more by emotion than anything else. They do have good judgment and can understand others, but the passion in which this individual feels emotion can be overwhelming at times. There are high senses of jealousy and even possessiveness with this individual.

## Moon in Sagittarius

Sagittarius is ruled by Jupiter, the planet of good fortune. Jupiter and the Moon share a friendly relationship, and they balance each other out. Thus, the Moon in Sagittarius is likely to be very balanced as well. They are both spiritual and intellectual as well. They are known for their sense of justice and seek out freedom. As a good learner and listener, this native is likely to be very easy to get along with. They are strong at making decisions and tend to be very optimistic with how they approach life around them. However, sometimes, they can also be too idealistic at times. These individuals can be great friends to others as well and are good friends.

*Moon in Capricorn*

Capricorn, ruled by Saturn, is not a very good placement. This placement creates an inimical relationship, and as a result, the individual is likely to suffer from delays and obstacles throughout their time. This individual, however, does get some benefits as well. They get benefits such as being determined, persistent, and resolute; these are qualities thanks to Saturn's reign over Capricorn. These individuals are known to be quite stubborn and difficult to manage. They are known for being serious and difficult at times, but they also bring with them stability.

They work hard for their lives to do what they would like to do. They are emotional internally, but being able to express themselves comes difficult to them. They feel self-conscious oftentimes, and they cannot find it in themselves to express themselves. Conservative by nature, they tend to struggle sexually as well. They cannot bring themselves to tell others what they need. However, on the positive side, they tend to reach great success in life.

*Moon in Aquarius*

Aquarius is ruled by Saturn as well. Due to the inimical relationship between the Moon and Saturn, this position is difficult. There are some natural obstacles that build up with this particular placement on the natal chart. This individual is likely to have a very fertile imagination, on the other hand, and can even be revolutionary. This individual is known for being able to observe and analyze well and is able to do so without getting too attached. They come across as impersonal to everyone they do not know but still feel strongly within themselves. They believe that justice is necessary and work hard to make sure of it. They crave adventure and changes in pace whenever possible, and anything other than that can be problematic. Unfortunately, however, their intense emotions can sometimes lead to addiction to drugs or alcohol.

*Moon in Pisces*

Pisces is ruled by Jupiter and is known to be a very emotional sign. It is even more emotional when enhanced by the Moon. Jupiter and the Moon share friendly relationships with each other. These individuals can be quite determined to create high expectations for themselves as well. They create situations in which they struggle to find peace mentally due to the fact that they struggle to actually meet those impossibly high standards. Their emotions become overwhelming almost, and they even start to pick up on the emotions of others as well, thanks to their intense intuition. These individuals tend to connect strongly with others, even without having to speak a word out loud. They tend to be quite polite, and this brings them plenty of happiness.

**Mercury**

Mercury is an incredibly important sign in your chart. In this case, it is responsible for creating the foundation of your personality. This planet is the closest one to the Sun and is very personal. Mercury is best in Air signs, but in fire signs, it may create a native who is going to be impulsive. In a water sign, Mercury is likely to create a native who is emotional rather than logical. Finally, in earth signs, it creates effects where someone is an overly cautious thinker. Now, let's go over all of the signs to determine the effects.

## Mercury in Aries

As a fire sign, Aries can be good but somewhat contradictory as well. Aries is ruled by Mars, and the relationship between Mars and Mercury is one that changes up effects. These people tend to be wise and smart. They typically are quick-witted and able to debate well, especially with their tendency to be argumentative. They are rarely willing to hesitate and, as a result, can be quite skilled in getting what they want. They are determined and will work hard to get what they want. They are quick-witted, quick at learning, and quite interested in music and physical pleasures. They are typically very willing to get their work done sooner rather than later, and as a result, they do not delay. They will meet their deadlines and communicate well as well. However, they may find themselves fickle and immoral at times.

## Mercury in Taurus

Mercury in Taurus, brings together the neutrality of Mercury being earthy with the earthiness of Taurus as well. Together, they create people who are very difficult to sway, who are going to be very firm in their views. You will not be able to budge these people once they have made their decisions, and as a result, they are difficult to push into doing what you want them to do. They are also generally quite lucky and are stable as well. They are generally stable, able to concentrate, and dependable in life. They particularly excel in business and money management. However, they also have a love for satisfaction, comfort, and beauty.

## Mercury in Gemini

As Gemini is an air sign and is ruled by Mercury, Mercury in Gemini becomes a very good placement. This particular placement tends to create positivity thanks to the fact that these two signs end up working together. When you are native to this combination, you will find that you get very good benefits. This native is likely to be very well-versed in communicating and articulating themselves with others. This helps them immensely, and thanks to it, they also start excelling in math, accounts, language, and similar. They can learn a lot and also gain the recognition that they will need to help them to achieve the success that will help them to get that beneficial affluence they want. They quickly get to find solutions to their problems thanks to their intellectual prowess.

*Mercury in Cancer*

In the mutable water sign of Cancer, Mercury is tied to moodiness. Cancer is ruled by the Moon, which brings with it those uncontrolled emotions. This is important—the moodiness of Cancer is sort of balanced out by the neutral Earth sign of Mercury. Together, they create deep emotions, but those which are very focused and stabilized. This person tends to be wise and able to channel their emotions as necessary. Mercury in Cancer tends to create deep philosophizers. They are emotional but also strong in mind to keep themselves on track.

This native is able to memorize information quickly and tends to use that to help them listen more as well. They have vivid imaginations and tend to trust their intuition. They are sentimental, loyal, and loving, and they find themselves communicating readily.

*Mercury in Leo*

Mercury in Leo, is a good combination. This placement is beneficial thanks to the fact that the Sun is the Lord of Leo, and

Mercury and the Sun are friends. This means that together, they work quite well. Thanks to Mercury's control over communication and the strength of Leo, this native is someone who becomes very mature and kingly in their manner. They are refined and yet also bold at the same time. They have a way to command the people around them, and they are quite intelligent at the same time. They have this power that will help them in most aspects of their lives.

These natives tend to be strong and very well successful in life. They are able to make the efforts to make sure that they get those benefits. They tend to do best as leaders and as people who are able to bring more support to others. Their personality and disposition tend to be stronger, and that is really important to acknowledge. They thrive in positions of authority, such as being a politician or administration.

*Mercury in Virgo*

Mercury, when in Virgo, is a duel earth sign. It is a combination of the earthy Virgo and the earthy Mercury. This creates exalting, and that allows for positivity. The energy that is created by Mercury then affords that native with the rationality necessary and the approach of practicality. This person tends to be careful and is strongly suited to business. Their actions are typically backed by a degree of acute attention to detail, and that helps them, especially with their observation and analytical abilities.

This person is going to be best suited to intellectually stimulating and challenging environments, and that helps them to become skilled in most situations. They typically thrive as teachers, accountants, or other similar people. Mercury in Virgo allows for stronger communication skills, and that makes them thrive in most of their situations.

*Mercury in Libra*

Libra is a mutable air sign, ruled by Venus. Because both Venus and Mercury are friends, Mercury in Libra is actually beneficial. When you see this sign combination, you get a position that is auspicious for the native. This puts together the effect of someone who is able to communicate well and is quite sophisticated thanks to the energy from Venus. However, the earthiness from Mercury helps to even it out. These natives may speak lavishly but are also driven toward building good, solid relationships. If you are born under this sign, you will find yourself quite gifted in persuasion.

*Mercury in Scorpio*

Scorpio is a fixed water sign and is indicated by heightened emotions, passion, and ambition. The Scorpio sign creates high levels of emotionality and passion, but that comes with its passion as well. However, the placement is not the greatest. When you are native to this combination, you will see that there are issues with the individual being able to connect to others. While it is important for you to be able to communicate well, there are issues with secretive attitudes for these people. They are probing and even inquisitive at times. But, they also may come across as harsh, to the point of aggressive at times. They must be mindful of the fact that they may be deemed problematic sometimes. While the Moon in Scorpio creates passion, Mercury grounds that passion as well to help sway the individual. They will do what they can to do what they believe is right and think very highly of themselves.

*Mercury in Sagittarius*

Sagittarius is a fire sign that is ruled by Jupiter. Jupiter itself is highly regarded as being a benefic planet, and that helps immensely with it. Despite the relationship between Jupiter and Mercury being less than stellar, in this placement, there are positive results created due to the benefic nature of both planets. People with this combination tend to be quite liberal in life and enjoy being diplomatic and sometimes even spiritual. They are well-read and are driven to understand people, cultures, and languages.

## Mercury in Capricorn

Capricorn is a mutable Earth sign that has Saturn as its lord. While Saturn and Mercury may be on good terms, it is important to recognize that this placement tends to create obstacles as well due to the omnipresence of Saturn in the background. Mercury in Capricorn tends to create people who are quite methodical and even cautious at times. They want to be certain that they make the right decisions and, as such, tend to think before acting. Both Capricorn and Mercury, being Earth signs, tend to be very grounded, creating a steady root in realism.

Typically, these people will possess high levels of prowess in business and organization, and they are excellent at being able to navigate through these situations.

## Mercury in Aquarius

Aquarius is a fixed air sign that is ruled by Saturn. Mercury in Aquarius creates people who are almost the opposite of those born under Mercury in Capricorn. They are typically very distractible and tend to brag a lot. They get lost in their minds more often than not, and because they feel like their minds are racing, they can wind up in a position where they are stuck in negativity. They can get caught up in innovative thoughts and actions at times, but that can also create issues for them as well. They are typically emotionally detached, but they still manage to help others when they are in positions of needing help.

## Mercury in Pisces

Thanks to its position with Jupiter as its lord, Pisces is a dual water sign. It, when combined with the Earthy and neutral toward Jupiter Mercury, creates a situation in which Mercury is actually debilitated. This position, however, is not entirely awful; both Planets are benefic in nature, so even when they are clashing with each other, they are still able to work together well. They can be excessively sensitive at times, so they can wind up getting hurt relatively quickly as well. They try to see the good in everyone and will trust too soon as well. However, they are also gentle and polite and tend to feel drawn to beautiful things. Mercury in Pisces tends to create dreamers.

**Venus**

Venus is the planet that controls your relationship. It is linked to your happiness and love. It determines how you find enjoyment in life, as well. Typically, this sign becomes relevant once you start finding love in your life. It also controls what you want out of your partner as well as how you are likely to connect to those partners that you have. It will also have control over what happens on your end in relationships as well. How you behave in your relationships will fall under Venus's rule.

*Venus in Aries*

Aries, ruled by the fiery Mars, is also a fiery sign. Venus and Mars share a neutral relationship with each other. The watery Venus, when in such a fiery sign, actually helps to create an assertive individual who is able to fully express their love. They may be careless at times in their love life, and they may not sugarcoat their emotions. However, their need for honesty creates the occasional aggressive conflict due to the fact that both of these Planets are passionate and sensual. Their high levels of energy often lead to the creations of high levels of libido as well, and those can sometimes cause issues. These individuals tend to be ruled more by their need for materialism than their religion. They prefer to enjoy the corporeal pleasures of life.

*Venus in Taurus*

Taurus is ruled by Venus, so placing Venus into Taurus is a very good spot for it. This particular position creates an individual who is attractive and beautiful, thanks to the power of Venus, and is also quite independent. They are drawn in by nature and pleasures in life and prefer to maintain their own autonomy. They are refined and enjoy their ability to connect to those that matter to them. They want stability more than anything else, and they make sure that they spend time being loyal to make sure that they keep those relationships with others.

*Venus in Gemini*

Gemini is ruled by Mercury, which is friendly with Venus. When you bring together the airiness of Gemini with the wateriness of Venus, you create a bubbly personality. This sign creates childlike and sometimes even childish individuals who want to make the most out of their lives. They love enjoying things as much as possible. They tend to be very open to relationships but can even become quite impatient and even fickle sometimes.

This native is likely to remain in an excitable mood often, but they also struggle with the maturity that they need in life as well. They tend to have a childish approach to romance as well, and that can be a problem for them. They tend to be overly optimistic early on, and they tend to approach their relationship with hope and expectations for love. However, this can be problematic for them. They cannot contain their emotions most of the time and find that they get into trouble. They may find that they have issues with their friendships and may overthink things sometimes, causing issues in their relationships as well.

## Venus in Cancer

Cancer is a water sign that is ruled by the Moon. The Moon and Venus, however, have a very inimical relationship. People born under this placement are heavily swayed by the water element thanks to the combination of the watery Cancer, the watery Venus, and the watery Moon. They tend to be very emotional and sensitive, as well. They usually find themselves getting attached to other people quickly, and they are especially vulnerable in their relationships as well due to the fact that they are easily sweet-talked.

Venus in Cancer creates people who are wise and strong, as well as virtuous and powerful as well. They thrive in their social and professional lives and tend to also be very artistic as well. They are usually struggling with their relationships with women and may find that they are very moody and even unpredictable at times. They need to try to be strong emotionally, but they may sulk instead.

## Venus in Leo

Leo is ruled by the fiery Sun and is a fiery sign as well. Venus and the Sun are inimical together. However, this doesn't create a negative placement due to the fact that the Sun is generally influential. The fire and heat of the Sun tend to start evaporating away the energy from Venus and creates a much more balanced individual. Those born with Venus in Leo tend to be stable, warm-hearted, and compassionate. They tend to be strong at self-expression, and Venus tends to give them more creative energy that they can use. The Sun gives them the confidence to act upon it. These people are mostly fulfilled by love. They are drawn toward finding those dating rituals and are always loyal to their loves.

## Venus in Virgo

Virgo is ruled by Mercury. However, Venus is debilitated by Virgo as well. Despite that debilitation, this is an average position due to the fact that Mercury and Venus are friendly toward each other. However, there are negativities that carry over toward marriage and their partnerships. Generally speaking, this native is usually cautious and careful in their lives. They crave love and attention from their partners, and they are constantly thinking about how they can get their love. They delve into love and devote themselves to it. They love luxury and enjoy physical and material goods, and are attracted to beauty.

*Venus in Libra*

Libra is lorded by Venus. Thus, Venus in Libra is a very comfortable position for the individual. Venus is a feminine watery planet, and Libra is mutable and airy. The combination creates bubbly energy. These individuals tend to be very influenced by their surroundings. They feel a strong need for love and relationships and prefer to function with other people. They usually are quite skilled in being able to communicate with other people. They are very romantic and emotional. As such, they tend to fall in love with other people often. They feel a strong need for love from others, and when they do not have it, they struggle. They spend their life trying to get that happily ever after marriage, and they are very serious about achieving that love and romance from others. They do whatever they can to preserve their relationships, and that sometimes comes at a cost.

*Venus in Scorpio*

Scorpio is a watery sign that is ruled by Mars. The neutral relationship between Mars and Venus works here and creates a native who is strongly associated with both passion and sensuality. When Venus is in Scorpio, it tends to relate to an individual who is very aggressive and even assertive at times. This individual is likely to find their fulfillment through their own assertiveness in love matters. The influence of Mars over Venus creates aggressive approaches to love, and these individuals tend to be both loyal but also bitter and driven by revenge if they feel like they have been betrayed.

*Venus in Sagittarius*

Sagittarius is ruled by Jupiter, and Jupiter and Venus are inimical in their relationship. This enmity between them, however, maintains its auspicious influence because Jupiter is a very benefic planet, and Venus is also benefic. Those with this placement find that they have a very good life financially. They are dutiful and help readily. People like this help others and feel the most comfortable when they are around people that they trust. They are very sociable and lucky as well. These natives do whatever they can to make their family proud and love to better themselves. They also have a fondness for decorating things as well.

*Venus in Capricorn*

Capricorn is a movable Earth sign and is ruled by Saturn. This creates a degree of stability to the temperament created by the individual. They tend to be very reserved and emotionally bottle things up. These individuals struggle with expressing their emotions and may struggle to tell their partners what they want in life. They tend to be very timid in their relationships and are insecure as well. They typically find themselves running away from their problems when they have them, and that can actually cause them issues as well.

*Venus in Aquarius*

Aquarius is also ruled by Saturn. The neutral airiness of Saturn connects to Venus well, thanks to the fact that both Venus and

Saturn are friendly with each other. Saturn is a guide that is also known for creating obstacles along the way. When Venus is placed with Saturn, the individual ends up being quite detached from romance. Their love life is usually a bit more difficult than that of the average individual, and those with this placement have very little regard for their friends, family, and the society that they live within.

These natives value and require their own personal space due to their need for autonomy. They usually follow their own rules the way that they want to. Their attitude is typically much calmer than one would expect, and their personality is quite good as well. They have a good, solid, and open approach to their lives, and they understand their relationships. However, they usually get married much later than most.

*Venus in Pisces*

Venus is exalted in Pisces and naturally finds that it gets great positive results. Due to the influence of the water element, this individual tends to be very deep and flexible. They can be very moody as well sometimes, but also may find that they stop and become almost depressed at times. They will suffer in silence rather than voice that they have an issue. This individual submerges themselves in romance and tends to be very polite and attractive. They tend to earn wealth in life.

Venus in Pisces creates an accommodating and even flexible individual. They are able to bend to just about any situation that they are in. Especially in their love lives, they will find that they are constantly trying to fit with it. They are terrified of rejection, and because of that, they constantly try their best to keep their partner happy. They need to be loved and understood, and they need a partner who is able to control and tame their emotions.

## Mars

Mars is a masculine planet that creates raw energy. It is the ability to create aggression and courage in the individual. It creates competitiveness, adventurousness, and assertiveness. It gives you an idea of what your most basic desires look like. It is the action in your life and the way that you approach all goals in your life. It will dictate your immediate response when you must act without thinking, and it represents the libido as well.

### Mars in Aries

In Aries, Mars is at home. This position creates strong, sturdy individuals with a tendency toward aggressive endeavors at times. They are very fond of physically demanding activities and thrive in the military. They are generally very innovative as well. These natives love a life of adventure and are very decisive. They prefer speed and can be very argumentative as well. While they are adept at debates, they sometimes struggle with their tendencies to lash out at others thanks to their aggressive instincts. These people are very easy to read and straightforward—what you see is what you get.

### Mars in Taurus

Taurus is ruled by Venus, a feminine and watery planet. Venus and Mars have a neutral relationship due to the conflicting values they represent. Mars, when placed in a stubborn sign with a delicate planet, becomes somewhat contradictory. Mars will not have as much activity due to this. People with this sign placement tend to be low in physical energy. They are, however, incredibly skilled in mental concentration. They learn a lot about the world based on the people around them and their experiences and mistakes that they make. They are very stable and determined, and they tend to dedicate themselves to beauty and the arts. They may even be quite artistic as well. Thanks to Mars, they have strong control over their ability to manage money and tend to be inclined toward feeling sensual. They are, however, usually unhappy in their relationships and marriages most of the time. They feel dissatisfied with their partner and may also become quite possessive or even violent at times.

## Mars in Gemini

Gemini is an air sign that is ruled by Mercury, the neutral earthy planet. However, due to the inimical nature between Mars and Mercury, there is a lot of contradiction here. The intellectual nature of Mercury convenes with the high energy of Mars, and the individual is usually active, logical, and skilled. They are strong in the arts and usually feel the need to travel. This placement creates a solid understanding of judgment and laws. This individual may feel drawn toward superficial romantic relationships and may have issues with how he or she tends to engage with others. These natives, however, have a habit of going for new experiences in romance. However, due to their restlessness, they jump from person to person. They are constantly preoccupied, and that can be agitating for them.

## Mars in Cancer

Cancer is a water sign ruled by the Moon, and Mars and the Moon are both friendly as well. This creates a decent placement of Mars in Cancer as well. This native is likely to value their physical energy more than their emotional fortitude. They tend to be very mentally strong thanks to the combination of the mental Moon and the powerful Mars. They must have some sort of outlet for their energy and tend to express it emotionally due to the influence of the Moon. They are not very demanding or assertive at all, instead of taking the route of compromise whenever possible. However, they will not budge on their beliefs when they are very resolute about them. They are serious about their ambitions and will be quite independent and hardworking whenever possible.

## Mars in Leo

Leo is ruled by the Sun, and thanks to the fact that Mars and the Sun are both friends, this is a very good placement. People with this placement tend to be very helpful and even generous at times. They are kind and understanding, and very clever as well. They are very good at knowing what to do and when to do it. They are natural leaders with the right kind of personality to back it up. They tend to be very clever and know how to make the most out of their capabilities. They love to travel and are endlessly energized. They are known for their willpower and confidence as well. They are proud of their sexual prowess as well.

## Mars in Virgo

Virgo is a dual earth sign that is ruled by Mercury. Mercury and Mars have an inimical relationship. While Mars is masculine and fiery, Mercury is neutral and earthy, relating to intellect. This native tends to pay attention to the details as well. He is likely to pursue sex strongly and is also likely to thrive in mechanical type fields. The influence from the steadfast Mercury helps to tame the aggression capable of Mars. This individual is likely to be sweet and plans things well. They are sometimes overly energetic and even argumentative at a time, thanks to the influence of Mars. Their struggle with tolerance is a huge problem for them.

## Mars in Libra

Libra is an air sign ruled by Venus. Thanks to the neutral relationship between Mars and Venus, this is a relatively neutral sign position as well. Together, the masculinity from Mars and the femininity from Venus come together to create someone who is charming and incredibly easy to get along with. This individual tends to be the crowd's favorite and is very affectionate, as well as blessed with solid communication skills as well. They are willing to compromise as well and have a relatively balanced temperament. Occasionally, one sign or the other will take control and change how the individual behaves. Mars in Libra allows for an individual who is very captivated with the arts and beauty. They are typically much more inclined toward their emotional side than their physical

*Mars in Scorpio*

Scorpio is ruled by Mars, making this a very comfortable placement. Mars will help greatly here, and this individual is likely to be very strong-minded and self-driven as well. They tend to rely on themselves without leaning on others. They typically have very high levels of energy, physically and mentally as well. They may not be very outspoken, however, and tend to be almost secretive. They are very attracted to those of the opposite sex and may even be jealous of others. They can become very possessive of their partners at the time and will always remember the wrongs. They are very loyal friends, but also horrible enemies if you cross them.

*Mars in Sagittarius*

Sagittarius is a fire sign that is ruled by Jupiter. Mars and Jupiter have a friendly relationship, making this position of Mars in Sagittarius also quite positive and friendly. Jupiter is the planet of luck, fortune, and growth, while Mars represents energy, passion, and ambition. Jupiter tends to lessen the levels of negativity from Mars and creates a native who is very strong mentally. This individual tends to be strongly aligned with justice, and they will stand up for their beliefs at all costs. They are reluctant to listen to the opinions of others, however. They are typically quite skilled in communication. They typically are skilled in writing as well. They have natural courage that they can use as well, and they are great in their adventures. They tend to make fantastic teachers and priests.

## Mars in Capricorn

Capricorn is ruled by Saturn. Due to the inimical relationship between Mars and Saturn, this individual is likely to face some serious troubles. They typically are loaded up with energy, but that energy is likely to be problematic as well. These individuals tend to be very harsh and sometimes even aggressive in nature. They are usually somewhat reserved in public areas, however, and they cannot resist indulging in gossip as well. This combination creates someone who has physical and mental strength but lacks the emotional depth that will allow them to build meaningful relationships.

## Mars in Aquarius

Aquarius is an air sign that is ruled by Saturn. Again, we are looking at the inimical relationship between the two. However, this is a more positive placement than Capricorn, thanks to the fact that Aquarius tends to be very humanitarian and even accommodating. This individual is likely to focus on their intellectual side of life, and they are usually skilled in the organization. They lead well and think well for those they lead as well. They are likely to love and emphasize justice and will look at freedom of speech as a benefit. This individual is stable and very dependable as well. They are the ones that everyone else trusts, and they are always looking for novelty.

## Mars in Pisces

Pisces is ruled by Jupiter, and Jupiter and Mars share a good relationship with each other. This combination creates a moral and spiritual individual who is willing to follow the straight and narrow. They tend to devote themselves to religion and religious beliefs, and they tend to be quite skilled in how they do so. They also have a sense of confusion sometimes, however, and their idealistic tendencies can cause issues for them. They tend to err on the side of sensitive and emotional.

## Jupiter

Jupiter is the largest planet in the solar system. It is an expanding planet in astrology as well. Anything that Jupiter touches it accentuates and expands further. This planet is considered the benefic planet and will create largely positive effects most of the time. Those with strong placements for Jupiter tend to thrive well in their lives.

### Jupiter in Aries

Aries, the fire sign ruled by the fiery Mars, creates an interesting combination. This combination, thanks to the friendly relationship between Mars and Jupiter, is quite positive for the native. This individual is likely to be somewhat argumentative thanks to the influence of Mars, but Jupiter also tends to rein it in somewhat, allowing for intelligence and logic to help temper the aggression. These individuals become strong in legal environments. They tend to be somewhat spiritual, compassionate, and generous as well. They usually enjoy donating to charities and religious places.

### Jupiter in Taurus

Taurus is ruled by Venus, the feminine and watery planet. Venus and Jupiter share a neutral relationship, but thanks to the benefic nature of Jupiter and the positivity of Venus, this combination is generally considered to be positive. These individuals tend to be broad in body and generally attractive. They are very religious and spiritual, and these natives tend to earn plenty of fortune in their lives. The placement of Jupiter allows them to gain the luck they need. These natives tend to be very wise and political. They are skilled in business and tend to be very conservative and even inflexible at times.

*Jupiter in Gemini*

Gemini is ruled by Mercury, and the two are both air signs. Mercury and Jupiter share an inimical relationship, however thanks to the benefic nature of both planets, this combination is quite good. This placement allows for the individual to be very wise and well-learned. They are skilled in studying, and even without formal education, they learn rapidly. They are driven toward discovering and learning new things, and that will help them to stay happier in their lives. They are open to new traveling locations and ideas.

Jupiter in Gemini makes the individual quite diplomatic- they have the ability to navigate through difficult situations tactfully. They are generally built quite tall, and as individuals, they are quite helpful to everyone around them. They devote themselves tirelessly to their work and tend to be incredibly dependable, taking their responsibilities seriously as well. They are pure, and they do well in learning about people. They are largely diplomatic in nature and tend to love interacting with other people in a tactful manner

*Jupiter in Cancer*

Cancer is ruled by the Moon. Jupiter and the Moon, being friendly, and with Jupiter being exalted in Cancer, this position becomes well balanced. This particular position is noted by the stabilized flow of emotional energy that comes from the Moon. When Jupiter is in Cancer, the native tends to be very good looking and is very intelligent as well. They are usually skilled at math in particular.

This individual tends to be very good-natured, generous, charitable, and loyal. They are likely to be wonderful friends and do what they can to help those they care about. They do indulge in gossip on occasion, but that can change up how they tend to provide for the people in their lives. They tend to be quite wealthy and accumulate money because they save well.

### Jupiter in Leo

Leo is ruled by the Sun, which is quite friendly with Jupiter. Though the Sun can be malefic at times, Jupiter's position in the Sun allows it to lessen the negative impact, so the fire from the Sun no longer burns as much. Instead, it provides a much-needed warmth to the individual. Thanks to the fact that both Planets are friendly toward each other, this placement becomes very favorable for the native. This placement creates an individual with high self-esteem and self-confidence.

This particular placement creates a strong leader, who may sometimes extend into having a superiority complex at times. This individual is likely to be very ambitious in their career and may also brag at times, in a dramatic way. They typically, however, tend to be quite charitable as well and are willing to help someone else in need if necessary.

### Jupiter in Virgo

Virgo is a dual earth sign, ruled by the earthy Mercury. However, Mercury and Jupiter both have an inimical relationship that is only set off by the fact that they are both benefic in nature. Their combination doesn't cause any negativity at all. In this position, Jupiter gifts the native with ambition, communication skills, and intelligence. They find themselves driven to succeed at just about anything that they start trying to do; they are also quite cautious with the approaches that they take to what they wish to achieve.

They tend to be practical, and they are willing to see details and demand proof before believing. They love nature and pure of heart, and they tend to be very generous with those around them. However, they do not give blindly—they only give when it feels practical to do so.

*Jupiter in Libra*

Libra is ruled by the watery Venus. Jupiter shares an inimical relationship with Venus, despite this, because of the benefic nature of Jupiter, the position tends to be good as well. People with this particular placement tend to be attractive, thanks to Venus's domain over beauty and the expansion that Jupiter provides. They tend to be interested in wealth and being polite. They are very well-mannered and tend to respect their guests. They also are quite religious, but also open-minded. They approach everything with a desire to see justice upheld, and they are attracted to those who are just as idealistic as these natives are. They tend to be quite beneficial to those around them, and they thrive well.

*Jupiter in Scorpio*

Scorpio is a fixed water sign that is governed by Mars. Mars and Jupiter are friendly toward each other, which means that the placement tends to be balanced. Scorpio tends to be vindictive and is not willing to forget when they have been betrayed, and Jupiter expands this. These individuals tend to be passionate and are determined to maintain secrecy when possible because they value privacy. However, they can also be quite diplomatic when treated fairly. They are proud and even selfish at times, and yet, they manage to do well in the financial field.

*Jupiter in Sagittarius*

Jupiter is at home in Sagittarius, and that creates a benefic effect for the native. Jupiter, in this position, creates a natural inclination for spirituality and religion, and these individuals tend to want to do what will be the most beneficial to the people they are around. They love to earn, but they also love to be able to provide for others. These individuals tend to earn a lot of wealth in life, and they also tend to use their skills to help with it. However, they are charitable and love to teach and mentor others while also engaging in charity when possible. They tend to come out on top in difficult situations with luck on their side as well. They tend to be quite fond of business and religion and tend to be very influential to others.

## Jupiter in Capricorn

Capricorn is ruled by Saturn, the neutral airy planet. Saturn and Jupiter are both neutral toward each other, and this creates a negative effect on this placement. Additionally, Jupiter is debilitated in Capricorn and is unable to allow its positivity to come out due to the malefic impact from Saturn. They are highly ethical and disciplined, but they do run into many issues. They are highly ambitious and compassionate, but they also lack intelligence and tend to have to work harder in life.

## Jupiter in Aquarius

Aquarius is also ruled by Saturn, and again, this creates a malefic effect on the individual. However, this is a slightly better position than Capricorn for Jupiter, thanks to the fact that Aquarius is more accommodating. These individuals tend to be intellectual and love justice and diversity. They accept all people, regardless of social standing, and tend to be very compassionate and even tolerant, erring on the side of impartial and unbiased as much as possible. They are original and imaginative, and though they seem to be rather unapproachable, this is because they spend so long getting caught up in their own minds while daydreaming. They are very philosophical and meditative by nature and allow that to rule them. However, at times, it tends to create a negative effect as they do not always control it accordingly.

## Jupiter in Pisces

Jupiter is at home here with Pisces, making it a very positive placement for Jupiter. This sign creates a good inheritance and good wealth for these individuals. Typically, they are more medium height but still quite healthy, and they tend to love being in higher positions in life whenever possible. They tend to be political and even diplomatic at times. They tend to have to travel often as well.

Pisces are generally associated with the twelfth house, and those in this position tend to be highly spiritual. They have strong imaginations and tend to allow themselves to be highly virtuous as well. They are usually quite well-liked in their social circles and usually tend to attach their emotions and self-worth to their religious convictions.

## Saturn

The last planet that plays a role in your chart, Saturn marks the creations of restrictions and limitations. While Jupiter expands, Saturn limits. It is indicative of regulations, rules, authority, and even control. Typically, Saturn works much like justice and will create rules and policies that must be upheld, and it is responsible for the effect of karma on your life. You might try to surpass the limitations that Saturn creates, but all you will do is cause yourself issues. You must be mindful of what Saturn dictates and make sure that you don't try to push past it. When you limit yourself based upon what you see Saturn dictating, you will actually realize that Saturn acts as a sort of guardian for you—someone who is able to help you better yourself more and more. This planet will help to govern how you control your life. It shows the restrictions that you will face and how guilty you feel.

## Saturn in Aries

Saturn is highly inimical toward Mars, the planet lording over Aries. Additionally, Saturn is debilitated in this position, making this position incredibly unpleasant for the native. This is especially true if your placement is in the seventh house—the house related to marriage. This position may also lead to increased aggression, as well. Those with this position tend to find themselves not enjoying contentment in their relationships with others. They are constantly faced with obstacles that get in their way, and this can cause significant anxiety and stress for them. They may have the ability to lead, but they often suffer as well due to misunderstandings and sometimes, even due to the fact that they can err on the side of overly indulgent, especially in illicit activities.

## Saturn in Taurus

Saturn and Venus are both very friendly, and as a result, Saturn is favorable in Taurus. This position creates those who are torn between trying to focus on their spiritual liberation and their material existence. They struggle with their desire for emotional and financial security. Saturn tends to make this individual very cautious, especially about money, and creates a thrifty native who will only spend when necessary. They tend to be very patient and disciplined and work hard to achieve the success that they want. They are usually quite clever and well-suited for the professions that put them talking with others. They thrive in politics and business, and the influence of Taurus also allows them to even become a bit sensual as well. They can succeed well in love, thanks to the influence of Venus.

## Saturn in Gemini

Mercury lords over Gemini, and Saturn and Mercury are almost friendly. Here, Saturn influences the judgment of the individual. These people may be deceptive at times and are also quite vulnerable to addiction as well. They tend to be mean and selfish at times and may also wander often. They lack stability and organization in life and tend to lead a very messy lifestyle. They may also be very narrow-minded as well, and though interested in science and logic, they may find themselves limiting themselves if something doesn't catch their attention. However, they are typically found to have good problem-solving and critical thinking skills and can control themselves when in difficult situations as well.

*Saturn in Cancer*

Cancer is ruled by the Moon, and Saturn is quite inimical toward the Moon. The end result is a native who faces some degree of mental distress to the native thanks to this placement. Those with this placement tend to have a great depth of character and thoughts that are profound and deep. Saturn allows them to reflect plenty, but the negativity of Saturn can also cause them to become quite depressed as well. They may expect a lot from others and get hurt when they realize that their expectations are not being met. They struggle when they are alone and do not enjoy peace of mind. They are lonely internally, though their external demeanor remains calm.

*Saturn in Leo*

Saturn in Leo creates a negative effect. Leo is ruled by the Sun, and the Sun shares an inimical relationship with Saturn. As a result, the native is likely to be very aggressive and not take their relationship with other people very well at all. They struggle with authority and tend to prefer to be the authority figure or to live alone. They don't want to be held back by others.

Saturn in this position creates a medium height, and someone who is quite stubborn. They work hard and work toward the leadership role that they desire. They tend to be very skilled and able to carry the load of work that they have without much struggle. They know that they want to be talented but struggle with expressing themselves well. They typically are quite loyal and don't play with other's emotions.

*Saturn in Virgo*

Virgo is ruled by Mercury. Saturn in Virgo creates an individual who is likely to be very crafty. However, despite that craftiness, he may struggle with being able to become the self-reliant person that he knows he can be. This native tends to have just a few friends but is loyal to them all. However, this person can also be somewhat quarrelsome at times and may cause issues with rudeness. Despite this, he is likely to thrive in situations where he is trying to be successful. He is likely to create the success he needs through careful and strategic planning. These natives know not to sweat the little things and tend to drive forward toward success with plenty of hard work.

*Saturn in Libra*

Libra is ruled by Venus, and again, Venus shares a friendly relationship with Saturn. Additionally, Saturn is exalted in Libra and, as such, is a very good placement for Saturn. Here, Saturn creates many successes for the natives and will allow them to thrive. They may show a tendency to collect material comforts and pursuits, but they also tend to understand the idea of balance in life as well.

Having Saturn in Libra creates a very justice-driven individual who seeks out fairness whenever possible. They tend to be great at cooperating with others and are very diplomatic, and are able to know how to use people to everyone's advantage. They tend to look great, but they also struggle in love due to feeling unloved and even ignored at times. A successful marriage with this person requires lots of patience and hard work.

*Saturn in Scorpio*

Scorpio is ruled by Mars, which shares an inimical relationship with Saturn. People with this particular placement tend to love diving into what they think about. They are deep contemplators, and sometimes, this can even lead to a reclusive nature due to the need to be on their own with their thoughts. They are typically reserved and serious but also strong-willed as well. They are curious and will attempt to decipher everything. Saturn in this placement will create a lot of aggression as well as a dominant personality. These individuals are big risk-takers who love adventures. However, sometimes, they find that their health issues hold them back. They are known for being prone to aggression and have a very strong drive for success.

*Saturn in Sagittarius*

Sagittarius is a sign ruled by the benefic Jupiter. Jupiter and Saturn are neutral toward each other. Jupiter helps with removing impurity while Saturn helps. Saturn allows Jupiter to overpower, and the individual becomes quite harmonious and even spiritual at times. This individual is quite serious and hard working. They tend to be smart, sincere, and also disciplined. They will focus on getting successes and will usually become quite popular. They will be generally happy in life and have good marriages and happy children.

*Saturn in Capricorn*

Saturn is at home in Capricorn, and this placement creates a very good one. This individual is going to be largely resilient and hard working. They are largely ambitious and will work past the delays that Saturn brings, being patient and willing to wait for the end result. They are usually fond of traveling and arts, with plenty of ambition and power as well. They value their careers greatly and are largely dependable and pleasant to be around. However, sometimes, they are suspicious and even selfish at times.

*Saturn in Aquarius*

Saturn rules Aquarius, and that allows for this to be a mostly positive placement as well. This placement allows for the individual to be flexible, but they also tend to contain a lot of emotions as well. They are very flexible and love justice, and are very compassionate. They tend to serve others and show that they have a solid understanding of what is right and wrong. They are usually strong leaders and will usually have a varied social circle. This placement creates natives who push for equality. They tend to be practical as well and work hard to better other people in their lives. They are impartial and pay attention to both sides of the argument to make sure they've got a rational decision. These individuals are usually quite responsible and great friends as well.

*Saturn in Pisces*

Pisces is ruled by Jupiter, and Jupiter and Saturn are both neutral toward each other. This creates a relatively neutral placement as well. These individuals are typically quite devoted to their spirituality and also work toward spiritual liberation. They are deep thinkers who tend to study everything they can. They focus on how to make better judgments and work well as mentors. They are usually sacrificing and are willing to do whatever they can for their loved ones. They are typically polite, compassionate, loyal, attentive, and even wealthy, with plenty of desire to continue earning. They tend to have a strong affinity for creative fields and love to work in either art or spirituality. They may also sometimes be indulgent as well.

## Rahu

Rahu is the north node of the Moon. Remember, the north node is the point of intersection between the Sun and the Moon, commonly referred to in Hindu mythology as the head of the Dragon. This is everything that directly defies the accepted norms of society. This planetary figure is very rebellious and fights against the authority figures. This is exactly why it does not mesh well with the Sun. It is deceptive and mysterious at times. This sign also is able to directly reflect upon your addictions that you may develop.

### *Rahu in Aries*

Rahu in Aries, a fiery masculine planet ruled by Mars, creates a negative reaction. Typically, the airy nature of Rahu fans the flames of Mars and makes this individual that much more aggressive. They tend to be aggressive and even reckless at times. They are always ready to fight and do not think about what may happen if they were to do so. However, they are clever and are very intelligent as well. They usually come into wealth at some point relatively unexpectedly, and they are driven by their need to succeed. They are very determined in their personal lives, and their career typically ends up progressing due to the amount of work that they put into it. They are short-tempered, and this causes all sorts of issues for them at work. They are sometimes selfish, harming their relationships. However, all things considered, this placement is still somewhat average.

### *Rahu in Taurus*

Rahu is exalted in Taurus, bringing positive results. This allows for stability to be brought to the individual's life. In this position, Rahu is associated with marrying someone of the opposite caste. These individuals tend to be recognized and respected by those around them. This individual is known for being wealthy and owning land. However, sometimes, they err on the side of short-tempered and even emotional at times. They tend to be argumentative sometimes just for the sake of arguing. They may be prone to addictions and may also work in fields that are considered unscrupulous.

*Rahu in Gemini*

Ruled by Mercury, Gemini is a positive placement for Rahu. Rahu and Mercury both are airy and work well together. Rahu in Gemini creates an individual quite skilled in a wide range of fields and is also skilled in being mysterious and able to manipulate others. Mercury is associated with wisdom and intelligence as well, creating a tactful individual capable of solving any problems that arise. However, Rahu also causes stress for the native as well. They are clever, but they sometimes get caught up in trying to figure out what they can do to protect themselves. They get so busy and so caught up in their thoughts that they can't slow down their minds.

*Rahu in Cancer*

Cancer is watery, and when Rahu is placed in a water element, it tends to become emotional but caring as well. With this combination, the Moon, the lord of Cancer, creates issues for Rahu. The emotions felt thanks to the Moon can be overwhelming and cause issues for the individual. These people tend to be a bit indecisive thanks to their wavering faith in themselves and their wavering thoughts. However, these individuals tend to be wealthy and authoritative, even in childhood. They struggle to connect to their mothers, and disputes in property are likely to occur. They may betray others and enjoy manipulating the emotions of others.

## Rahu in Leo

In Leo, Rahu creates negativity. This is because Rahu and Leo are inimical with each other—when they meet, they tend to create negative energy. Rahu adds to the aggression present thanks to the fiery Leo, and this can cause problems with these individuals. They may be driven to be recognized for their beliefs and ethics, but they struggle sometimes. They tend to detach from their families and clash with their fathers. They are great at strategy, however, and they have an impressive mind. They tend to be quite intelligent, but sometimes even shrewd. Their egos and self-interest are typically higher, and they may run into issues with children.

## Rahu in Virgo

Virgo is ruled by the airy Mercury. Thanks to the airiness of Rahu as well, this creates a comfortable position. The relationship between Mercury and Rahu is positive, and Rahu's airiness pushes the native higher and higher, while Virgo's earthiness keeps them grounded as well. This individual tends to thrive well in management and has a strong desire to be recognized.

These individuals tend to have a lot of courage and determination in their lives. They want to be able to succeed, and they usually manage to do so. However, they may struggle with their health and communication as well. They tend to face challenges head-on and have the skills fit for a politician as a result. These individuals tend to be in their element when they are in the government.

## Rahu in Libra

Rahu in Libra is relatively balanced out. Libra's desire for balance tends to influence the manipulativeness that comes with Rahu. Rahu creates the ability for the natives to be skilled in their manipulation while also being quite capable of creating balance in life as well. In this particular placement, Rahu is likely to create a detachment from elders in the native's family. They may lose land and may struggle in their marriages as well. These individuals tend to be destructive and almost aggressive and dominating in their relationships, and they do not trust their lovers. Because of this, they are constantly facing a degree of dissatisfaction with their love life. They are also typically prone to moral depravity at the same time as well, and that can be highly problematic for them.

*Rahu in Scorpio*

Scorpio, ruled by Mars, is inimical toward Rahu. The influence that Scorpio has toward secrecy and mystery layers along with Rahu's need for confidentiality, and the result is someone who is incredibly secretive. It is hard to know what they are doing and why. This tends to give the native the ability to be intuitive and capable of keeping secrets. However, this native tends to struggle with their health as well. They tend to feel very burdened, and they struggle to stay healthy. They tend to be very wealthy and strong, but they commonly find themselves using their strength and wealth for the wrong reasons rather than being productive. They love shortcuts and may also err on the side of antisocial at times.

*Rahu in Sagittarius*

Sagittarius is a sign of wisdom and is ruled by Jupiter, also related to Jupiter. This sign, with Rahu in it, allows for a good placement that is meaningful and indicative of being spiritually liberated. This individual strives to be the best in their education, and they want to be successful, but they also find themselves not really strongly believing in the spiritual realm. They are chasing after something that they don't believe. This individual is someone who wants to travel. They don't always get things that they want, and they have to learn.

## Rahu in Capricorn

Capricorn is ruled by Saturn, and Saturn and Rahu are friends. These two create a desire for leadership positions. Rahu brings stability to the individual's mindset. The individual is likely to be happy, strong, and even resolute, especially relating to their careers. However, they can also be somewhat wicked at times as well. They have a mind that drives them to get what they want. They like to achieve fame through their own efforts and are generally quite self-reliant as a result. They are generally quite capable of getting what they want, and sometimes, Rahu can leave this individual feeling confused at work.

## Rahu in Aquarius

Aquarius is ruled by Saturn. Both Saturn and Rahu are airy and create a positive influence. These individuals have very strong desires and aspirations, and they work hard to build. They worry about their social status and desire that social recognition. They want to be admired and respected, as well. This placement can cause problems with the individual's health as well. They also tend to struggle with their loved ones. They tend to focus on their wealth and earnings at home, and their willpower helps them to achieve their financial goals.

## Rahu in Pisces

Pisces is ruled by Jupiter. It is strongly associated with spirituality and intuition. Rahu in Pisces creates an imaginative world and plenty of depth to their thoughts and their spiritual and meditative tendencies. This placement of Rahu creates deep thinking for the native. Overall, this placement is generally just average. There may be problems in business, and they are likely to travel, but that travel was unwanted. Those born with this sign find themselves traveling regularly, and they work hard. However, they don't always get the payoffs for their work. They struggle with distress and sometimes feel entirely detached from their spouses as well, thanks to this placement.

## Ketu

Ketu is the southern node of the Moon. This is the point at which the Sun's path passes that of the Moon. This is the tail of the Dragon in Hindu mythology and is very similar to Mars. It is associated with illusion, detachment, liberation, and secrets. This particular celestial body is known for being malefic in nature. This particular planet aims for spiritual liberation, known as Moksha, and pushes the individual toward it.

### Ketu in Aries

Aries is a sign that is ruled by Mars, and it shares a good relationship with Ketu. Ketu tends to behave very similarly to Mars, and as such, this particular placement works out. There is a need for change and moving around, and these individuals can be somewhat moody at times. However, these individuals are also usually quite cheerful and are quite articulate as well. They prefer to live simple lives. They enjoy the calmness and need a quiet life. They tend to look for ways that they could live peacefully. They prefer not to be the center of attention, but they will put in plenty of effort to do whatever they need to do.

### Ketu in Taurus

Taurus is lorded by Venus, and Venus shares a very average relationship with Ketu. These people tend to prefer freedom to anything else. However, the earthiness from Taurus helps them to keep themselves grounded. They typically find that they are impulsive, and their steadfast Taurus nature tends to leave them struggling with themselves as well. They tend to desire stability while also wanting constant changing as well. They struggle with this, and they commonly also face issues with their romantic relationships as well. They tend to procrastinate and maintain stubbornness oftentimes, and this makes things difficult for them.

### Ketu in Gemini

Gemini, ruled by Mercury, creates issues for the individual. Ketu causes a feeling of double-mindedness. They feel confused and like they cannot find a resolution that they desire in life. They struggle to make decisions. They also tend to feel a strong need for freedom and struggle immensely when they find themselves restricted. Ketu in Gemini causes issues for the individual, leading them to be short-tempered oftentimes, which usually leads to all sorts of relationship issues as well. These people find themselves emotionally dissatisfied due to this. They are strong and sharp of mind, but they also tend to struggle with using it due to feeling unstable.

### Ketu in Cancer

Cancer, ruled by the Moon, is quite inimical toward Ketu. Ketu in Cancer is usually quite negative for the native—they are likely to struggle with their own relationships and commonly struggle to find a way to understand themselves and their own emotions. They tend to think of the negative possibilities more than the positive, and they usually doubt themselves regularly as well. This creates all sorts of misunderstandings and even obscurity. These individuals find themselves saddened and doubtful, and usually, they suffer from phobias as well. They are, however, also sympathetic to others and use that to their benefit.

### Ketu in Leo

Ketu in Leo is problematic. Leo is ruled by the Sun, and the Sun and Keto are harsh enemies with each other. The Sun creates aggression, and when Ketu is there as well, the individual becomes quite impulsive. They may be confused at times and usually find that they are easily frustrated. They do not like this degree of uncertainty, and it can cause a lot of doubt. These individuals tend to fear snakes and poison, and they are usually on the impatient side. They may be good at politics and tend to be quite independent.

## Ketu in Virgo

The earthy Virgo is known for creating observation, and when Ketu is added to this, the end result is mystery and secrecy for the native. They usually think deeply and analyze everything. They tend to be very talkative, and it creates a stable temperament for them. However, these individuals tend to procrastinate a lot as well, and that can be hugely problematic for them. They do live quite well because they are driven to achieve it and are quite smart, but sometimes, they struggle with finding the time to make it happen due to their preference and penchant for other types of activities.

## Ketu in Libra

Libra in Ketu creates balance. It creates a degree of airiness in which Ketu is able to influence the abilities to manage. This combination creates individuals who are very capable. They are aggressive and tend to be hard-working and sometimes even clever. They are talkative and skilled in public affairs. They thrive in the media and tend to be dominating at times. They are spiritual but may also be dishonest sometimes. This makes the native very dependent upon the family.

## Ketu in Scorpio

Ketu in Scorpio creates sharp mindedness. It is able to create skills in research. These individuals like to do things on their own. Scorpio is ruled by Mars, which enjoys a strong relationship with Ketu. Together, they create mystery and layers to one's personality. It is difficult to predict what those with this placement are thinking. They may be sharp-minded and even courageous. They give a strong determination, and they tend to throw themselves into their goals. This position creates talkative natures and people who are good at research. However, they may also be prone to cheating or taking advantage of others and can also be quite harsh at times.

### Ketu in Sagittarius

Sagittarius is good with management and leading. They tend to be quite skilled. As a result, thanks to Ketu, this individual aims to fly highly. They want to achieve great things, and they tend to have the fiery nature of Sagittarius controlled. This position is associated with spirituality. In this position, the individual is good with intuition. These individuals are strong leaders and tend to get great names to fame. They are intelligent as well. They tend to be carefree and even jubilant at times. They give a great temperament to the native. They are strong and have a need for freedom. They don't like being told what to do.

### Ketu in Capricorn

Capricorn is ruled by Saturn, which is on good terms with Ketu. This creates an individual that is strongly interested in social work and social causes. These individuals tend to accept what Saturn signifies, thanks to its friendliness. People with this placement tend to show strong interest in many new things. They also tend to be strongly accepting of others. They show interest in new things and tend to be very courageous. They are skilled in property and are very driven to achieve freedom in their lives. They tend to jump from job to job frequently and may get dissatisfied at times. They are usually fond of travel. They work hard and get strong positions of growth. The growth may be slow, but it is steady as well.

*Ketu in Aquarius*

Aquarius is ruled by Saturn as well. This particular placement becomes quite positive, as well. Those with this placement tend to be quite learned and recognize what is real in life. However, despite this, they tend to struggle to get what they want. Ketu in Aquarius gives desires to the individual. They also relate well to others. They tend to make plans that sometimes play out as unrealistic or even unnecessary. They often have ear-related issues and are very stubborn in nature as well. They will only change if they want to, and they struggle in familial and parental relationships.

*Ketu in Pisces*

This position is ruled by Jupiter. It is a sign of intuition and also imagination. When Ketu is placed within it, it creates individuals who are irresolute. They struggle to make decisions and have solid spiritual development. These individuals tend to be very meditative and even spiritually inclined at times. They tend to be dreamers who are commonly going to suffer from issues with the eyes and ears. They are typically fond of being able to travel and are very interested in religion. They are driven to achieve respect from others and are drawn toward a good position in society. They are humble individuals and are typically respectful of the position that they are in. They are very helpful and work to become skilled in their understanding of people. They respect their elders as well and are very knowledgeable as well.

# Chapter 9: Finding Your Partner With Vedic Astrology

In Hindu culture, it is not uncommon for people to engage in matchmaking, in which their horoscopes are used to help to create an understanding of the potential for connection between two people. Using one's birth chart, known as Kundli matchmaking, allows individuals to start seeing how compatible they are with their potential spouses. In this culture, it is recognized that marriage is planned even prior to birth, and it is written into the stars as well. Both the man and the woman's horoscopes are looked at to determine if there are any ill omens for the marriage. It is important to see where the issues may lie so there can be action taken in advance to try to sort of heal it, counteracting it. There are ways that couples can start overcoming the malefic effects, and that allows them to develop the solid relationship they need to have a successful marriage.

At the time of matching, there are several different aspects that come into consideration. The three primary factors are the Guna Milan, the Mangal Dosha, and the strength of the Navamsa Chart. This comes together to start looking at the potential for compatibility. Those skilled in matchmaking will go over all three of these factors to see how these aspects create a connection. Those who are highly compatible are likely to find great enjoyment in their marriages. They may not be perfect because no marriage is, they will be blessed with connection, love, and general positivity in their relationship. Their relationship will be overall quite harmonious. That is not to say that they will never argue—arguments happen when living in such close proximity to each other. However, it will allow the couple to be comfortable in their marriage with each other.

An unfavorable matchup creates a marriage that is likely to be very rocky and difficult to live through. There may be distrust or hatred or resentment present, or there may even be infidelity at times. It becomes difficult to find any sort of harmony for the individual. Their relationship becomes a point of contention.

## Guna Milan

Guna Milan is the process of Kundli matching. It involves checking several different combinations for compatibility. It is primarily done through software at this point due to the length of time that it takes to calculate it out. However, help you to understand the Ashtakoot Dosha for the individual—the several different aspects that influence marriage. Ashtakoot is a combination of "Ashta" for eight and "Koota," meaning aspects. Total, you get eight aspects to consider for marriage, and different points are assigned for each of them. The end result is that individuals have various compatibility with each other. The eight koota that are considered are Varna, Vashya, Tara, Yoni, Grahamaitri, Gana, Bhakoot, and Nadi. Each creates a different influence on the individual.

### Varna: Mental Compatibility

This creates a reading for the general compatibility for the individuals considering marriage. It takes a look at their general personality, skills, and abilities and takes a look at four key personality aspects as well and awards one point per category to determine whether these individuals are compatible. The four aspects of personality that are considered are:

1. Intellect, philosophy, and spirituality
2. Leadership, defenders of society, courage, and decisiveness
3. Business-mindedness
4. Work ethic and accountability

## Vashya: Power compatibility

This aspect starts looking at who is the most likely to be dominant in the relationship. Each of the partners will have a different personality type, and there are five possibilities that will help to figure out both dominance and compatibility. After all, two people who prefer to control everything are not likely to get along very well in marriage. Rather, they must have personalities that work well together. There can be up to two points awarded here, and they work in several ways. The five types of personality here are:

1. Individualistic with a preference for personal control and opinion
2. Domineering and powerful
3. Subservient
4. Accepting of power within a smaller scope of influence
5. Balanced and quieter in asserting power

## Tara: Health and general wellbeing

Tara will take a look at how healthy the spouses are. Those who are healthy together tend to have very strong, beneficial relationships without worrying so much about how well they work together. It could be good or bad, and depending upon it, it will be worth up to three points.

## Yoni: Physical and sexual compatibility

Yoni refers to the physical and sexual compatibility of the couple. Those who are compatible physically and sexually tend to do better. This is typically considered through identifying the sexual tendencies of both people, noting how the two interact. Each person is assigned an animal that is indicative of their own tendencies, and depending upon how compatible the two animals are, the individuals may or may not be very compatible. There can be up to four points scored here. The animals used include:

- Buffalo (Mahisha)
- Cat (Marjara)
- Cow (Gow/Gau)
- Deer (Mriga)
- Dog (Shwana)
- Elephant (Gaja)
- Horse (Ashwa)
- Lion (Simha)
- Mongoose (Nakula).
- Monkey (Vanara)
- Rat (Mushaka)
- Serpent (Sarpa)
- Sheep (Mesha)
- Tiger (Vyaghra)

**Graha Maitri: Progeny, affection, and harmony.**

This category generates up to five points between the two. It creates a picture of the likelihood of having children as well as what the mutual affection is likely to look like. It also considers the ways that individuals tend to view the world around them.

**Gana: Worldview**

The worldview that individuals take looks closely at the preferences that the individuals point to the world. They tend to focus on either spiritualism, materialism, or are balanced somewhere in the middle. When both are on the same plane, this can be worth up to six points.

**Bhakoot: Prosperity and love**

This considers just how likely two people are to be happy with each other, as well as influences the longevity of both partners. This is worth up to seven points.

## Nadi: Life force and health compatibility

Nadi relates to childbirth, love, and sensuality. When two people have the same Nadi, they cause defects, but there are ways to calculate this out and remedy the problem. This can create a score of up to eight Guna.

# Mangal Dosha

Mangal Dosha is known to be a drawback to one's charts. They are incompatibilities that must be remedied. When one or both partners are Manglik, then there may be struggles in the relationship. In particular, there are several negative effects of being a Manglik individual, but when both people are Manglik, the negativity tends to be canceled out. There are ways to remedy these incompatibilities as well that will help couples where one individual is Manglik as well.

Those who are Manglik tend to vary based on the different effects of the individuals. People with the Mangal Dosha tend to be very volatile and struggle in their relationships because they do not want to bend to their partners. Relationships are give and take—they must be approached as such as well. Additionally, the energy of these individuals is seen as fiery at times—the energy needs to be used the right way in the right direction, or it can become destructive. In terms of the married life, this individual may struggle mentally and see financial loss or ruin as well.

When the individual suffers from main Manglik Dosha, they are likely to suffer much more. This can even be deadly at times. It can lead to problems with the relationship between spouses, cause problems with one spouse dying, cause a major, debilitating accident, or cause disease as well.

## Effects of the Mangal dosha

The effects of the Mangal dosha vary greatly depending upon the placement of this combination. Their effects usually do not occur until after a wedding, meaning that many people may feel that they are compatible because they were prior to the true nature of the Manglik coming out. They are felt in the 1st, 2nd, 4th, 7th, 8th, or 12th house. When Mars is placed in any of these, there are negative effects thanks to the fiery nature of Mars.

Manglik dosha plays out in two types. There is the Anshik Manglik, translating to the "little Manglik," and there is the major Manglik dosh as well. Each of these will create various influences.

The Anshik Manglik usually ends after 18 years. They are generally resolved by Puja or other rituals that can be done. They are not strongly influential, but they do still push the individual and can be quite negative. They commonly create issues such as causing problems with health after the marriage ceremony, manifesting in small arguments between spouses, struggling in having children, and general tension.

Depending on where Mars is placed, the Manglik will have very different effects. They may find that they struggle in their relationships, or they might also have other issues with finances as well.

- **Mars in the 1st house:** When Mars is in the 1st house, the house of spouses, they normally see unnecessary conflicts in the marriage. The individual may also assault or be violent toward their spouse as well. Of course, this is entirely unacceptable, and as a result, the individual may suffer from tension, distress, or even be divorced due to the abusive nature of the Manglik.

- **Mars in the 2nd house:** When Mars resides in the 2nd house, the individual's family life is impacted greatly. They may struggle in their marriage to find any sort of harmony. They also may find themselves facing great obstacles, both in marriage and professionally as well.
- **Mars in the 4th house:** When Mars falls in the 4th house, there are major negative implications. In particular, this individual will struggle professionally and will usually jump from job to job on the regular. They are usually likely to face financial issues, and their general outcome is unhappy.
- **Mars in the 7th house:** This creates an individual who is highly irritable at all times. They generally have a sour temper and will also be very high in energy. They tend to get into fights thanks to their tendency to behave aggressively, and they struggle in their marriage because of it.
- **Mars in the 8th house:** This individual tends to be very lazy. They are careless and even sort of reckless in regards to their finances and assets. Most of the time, they end up losing property, especially that which they inherit from their parents.
- **Mars in the 12th house:** This individual tends to create enemies for the Manglik. They are likely to find themselves struggling mentally, and they may find themselves struggling in their relationships no matter what they try to do.

## Remedies

Thankfully, if one is Manglik, there are remedies that can be used to help to make sure that they can still enjoy a life that is full of happiness, and they can find enjoyment as well. When it is known that there are Mangal Dosha that must be addressed, the parties to the marriage can actively work to counteract them. Some of the strongest Mangal Dosha remedies include:

- Marriage between two Manglik individuals to nullify the effects.
- Fasting to help to satisfy and placate Mars.
- Mars is placed in the 1st house if Aries is also within this house.
- Kumbh Vivah—the process to marry with a pot to allow for the bad impact after their marriage life to be removed. This is one of the most common and significant solutions that you can use.
- Reciting mantras
- Offerings and contributions that are pleasing to Mars on Tuesdays, such as foods made out of red lentil, swords or knives, red silks, or other red stones.
- Wearing gemstone rings, specifically a golden ring with a red coral on the right ring finger.
- Visiting the Navagraha and Hanuman temples.

The most beneficial way to counteract the Manglik individual is to perform the Kumbh Vivah. With that ritual, the effects should be mitigated entirely.

## Navamsa Chart Compatibility

Finally, the last consideration during the matchmaking process is to watch the Navamsa charts of the individuals. It is important that both the ascendant and the 7th houses are compatible—if they aren't, there are serious issues that can be experienced. The 7th house is responsible for marriage and partnerships, including relationships of all kinds. As such, it becomes essential that the 7th house is compatible before marriage. Otherwise, there will be a significant problem.

With the ascendant, if there is a clash between the two intended spouses, there can be a mismatch in desire as well. This is hugely problematic if they do not align well—if you have one person whose Lagna is incompatible with the other, there is a very real possibility of issues.

Of course, the other Navamsa houses are important as well, albeit to a lesser extent. The 2nd house helps to determine the compatibility of happiness and the families that are coming together. The 4th house determines the happiness of the household that is being created by the newly married couple. The 6th house represents separation, litigation, and additional legal issues as well. The 8th house represents the longevity of marriage and determines just how well the couple will do together.

The 6th and 8th houses are both believed to be malefic, and they may impact the 7th or 4th houses and their lords, causing issues for the married couple.

Generally speaking, if either party has Mars, Sun, Rahu, Ketu, or Saturn in any of the Navamsa houses, there may be a significant mismatch in the ability to create a good, calm marriage. Especially if Mars, Sun, and Rahu are present, there is a higher likelihood of separation or divorce.

# Conclusion

When you get around in your life, you face a lot of unknowns. You may not know who your partner may be or what life might have in store for you. You may wonder why certain things happen to you or why you have to go through things that happen. The truth is, that you can learn. You can discover these secrets in your life if you are able to see what the stars have said about you at the moment of your birth.

Being able to understand the state of your fate means that you will be able to make decisions for yourself that you might not otherwise make. By being able to choose these out, you will be able to choose out the actions that will help you. You will be able to see what it is that the universe has in store for you. Learning to read this information in the skies means that you will get to understand so much more about what you can expect.

Looking at the stars is so beneficial to you. From being able to read the stars to understand your fate, to your compatibility with others, knowing what is written in your future has great benefits. As you read through this book, you were given so much information that would help you to understand yourself. It would help you to understand how to navigate. It helps you to see what it is that will happen in your life as well as what you can expect. When you start understanding why you are having certain struggles or challenges, or if you want to know what you can do to better work with your inherent strengths, this will give you that insight.

As you read through this book, you were given the tools that would help you to do so. However, just because you have read this book does not mean that you are done or that you are suddenly an expert in your chart. Understanding them will help you to start seeing the truth, but you will need to do more. You will need to reflect upon your understanding of yourself. You will need to stop and think about the understanding that you have built, and you will need to start thinking about the ways that it could have influenced your life. You will need to start listening to yourself and your intuition and then reflecting on what that could mean for you. Over time, you will start seeing the ways that it could influence you. You will start seeing that the universe, and your life, is complex.

Implementing the information that you have gained will help you to understand your life. However, having that understanding will make it so you have a better idea of how to pursue life. It will help you to start seeing what you can do and how you can use it to influence your own choices. As you start allowing yourself to go with the flow and to be the person that you want to be, you will realize that it is so much easier to do so. When you work on living true to yourself and to the fate that the stars have said, things get a bit easier.

So now, knowing what you know, you can start choosing to implement the knowledge that you have gained. You can start figuring out your own life. You can start trying to implement the knowledge to help others and to be the person that the Stars have told you that you will be.

From here, you may want to consider reading more into the combinations and how they can further influence the native. You may want to read more about the mythologies that come into play, or you may want to take a look at the Vedas themselves, reading them and absorbing the information. At the end of the day, you have so many options for information that can help you and all you have to do is make sure you know where to look.

Thank you for taking the time to read through this guide, and hopefully, you've found that the information is helpful to you.

# Conclusion

Hopefully, you've developed a better understanding of everything that you will need to know, and you are more driven to continue studying Vedic astrology and the Vedas. And, if it has been helpful, please consider heading over to leave a review!

www.ingramcontent.com/pod-product-compliance
Lightning Source LLC
Chambersburg PA
CBHW011318080526
44589CB00020B/2743